ENDOR~~~~~~~ ~ ~

"Like the book of Jude itself, this short commentary punches above its weight. Brumbach introduces the book and its author in an easily accessible way, drawing from the cutting edge of contemporary biblical scholarship. He also, from his own distinctive Messianic Jewish perspective, takes us to the heart of the text and its meaning for Israel and the nations.

—Dr. Richard Harvey, Associate Lecturer in Hebrew Bible and Jewish Studies and former Academic Dean, All Nations College, Hertfordshire, UK.

This book is a superb introduction to the Epistle of Jude that places the book's events, characters, and teaching in the Jewish world in which it was written. Rabbi Joshua Brumbach presents scholarly insights into the Epistle of Jude in an accessible, explanatory and uncomplicated manner, from a non-supersessionist point of view.

—Dr. Vered Hillel, Professor of New Testament Studies, former Associate Academic Dean, Israel College of the Bible, Netanya, Israel.

I am pleased to recommend this very well done commentary on Jude by Rabbi Joshua Brumbach. He has been careful with sources and restores Jude to the importance it should have in the Messianic Jewish and Christian communities.

—Dr. Daniel C. Juster, Director, Tikkun International, founding President of the Union of Messianic Jewish Congregations

Rabbi Brumbach presents a commentary that is not only enjoyable to read, in that it is clear, concise, and informative, but also offers an academic work that gives space for pastoral reflection. With use of current scholarship and rabbinic literature, he has presented an essential contribution to this series.

—Dr. Sophia Magallanes, Assistant Professor of Biblical Studies, Life Pacific College, San Dimas, CA

Bringing Jude's message to the church is a yeoman's task since it has been relegated to the end of the New Testament cannon by most of the translations. Rabbi Joshua Brumbach has produced a commentary that is both scholarly and readable. It should be required reading at every seminary.

—The Reverend R. John Perling, Mount Calvary Lutheran Church, Beverly Hills, CA

Rabbi Joshua Brumbach has given us more than a commentary on Jude. You will have the entire breadth of Second Temple Jewish literature opened to you in the most simple and clear manner.

—Rabbi Murray Silberling, Beth Emunah Messianic Synagogue, Agoura Hills, CA

A MESSIANIC COMMENTARY

From

JUDE

ON

FAITH AND THE DESTRUCTIVE INFLUENCE OF HERESY

A MESSIANIC COMMENTARY

From

JUDE

ON
FAITH AND THE DESTRUCTIVE
INFLUENCE OF HERESY

RABBI JOSHUA BRUMBACH

Lederer Books
A division of
Messianic Jewish Publishers
Clarksville, MD 21029

Copyright © 2014 by Joshua Brumbach

All rights reserved. No part of this publication may be reproduced, stored in a retrieval system, or transmitted in any form or by any means without the prior permission of the publisher, except for brief reviews in magazines, journals, etc. or as quotations in another work when full attribution is given.

The use of short selections or occasional page copying for personal or group study is permitted and encouraged, within reason. However, we ask that you respect the intellectual property rights of the author.

Unless otherwise noted, all biblical citations are from the *Complete Jewish Bible*, with minor alterations based on my own discretion to emphasize the underlying Greek, highlight a particular idea, or clarify the English translation.

ISBN: 978-1-936716-78-4
Library of Congress Control Number:

18 17 16 15 14   5 4 3 2 1

Published by
Lederer Books
A division of
Messianic Jewish Publishers
6120 Day Long Lane
Clarksville, Maryland 21029

Distributed by
Messianic Jewish Resources Int'l.
www.messianicjewish.net
Individual and Trade Order line: 800-410-7647

Email: lederer@messianicjewish.net

Printed in the United States of America

For my parents and family.
I am always grateful for your support.

I am incredibly grateful to my wife, Monique, a true Eshet Chayil, a woman of valor, who has always been my greatest support and closest friend. She read through every page and provided considerable feedback and input. It is really her encouragement that made this work happen. I am also grateful to our son, Gilad, who sacrificed playtime at the park while I worked on this book.

Special acknowledgement should also be given to Dr. Vered Hillel and Yahnatan Lasko who painstakingly reviewed the entire manuscript and offered considerable input, edits and corrections, as well as Benjamin Adelmann, Rabbi Dr. John Fischer, Rabbi Derek Leman and Dr. Kathryn Higuera Smith, who also contributed helpful comments and guidance. Their counsel greatly enhanced this work.

I would also like to thank the publisher, Rabbi Barry Rubin, and all those at Lederer/Messianic Jewish Publishers for their encouragement and guidance. You challenged me to expand what I wrote.

Additionally, I am indebted to the very few scholars who have already commented on the Epistle of Jude, especially Steven J. Kraftchick and Richard Bauckham. Only direct quotes and essential ideas are footnoted.

CONTENTS

GENERAL EDITOR'S COMMENTS

Nearly all bible commentators emphasize the importance of understanding the historical, cultural and grammatical aspects of any text of scripture. As has been said, "A text without a context is a pretext." In other words, to assume one can understand what God has revealed through those who present his word—prophets, poets, visionaries, apostles— without knowing the context is presumption. To really understand God's word, it's essential to know something about who wrote it and to whom, what was actually said and what it originally meant, when, where, and why it was written.

By now, everyone knows that the New Testament is a thoroughly Jewish book, written nearly entirely by Jews, taking place in and around Israel. The people written about— Paul, Peter, James, John, etc.—were almost all Jews who never abandoned their identities or people. The topics covered—sin, salvation, resurrection, Torah, Sabbath, how to "walk with God," the Millennium, etc.—were all Jewish topics that came from the Hebrew scripture. The expressions used often were Jewish idioms of that day. So, to fully understand the New

Testament, it must be viewed through "Jewish eyes," meaning that the Jewish historical, cultural, grammatical must be examined.

There are commentaries for women, for men, for teens, even for children. There are commentaries that focus on financial issues in the bible. Others provide archaeological material. Some commentaries are topical. Others are the works of eminent men and women of God. But, until now, no commentary series has closely looked at the Jewish context of the New Testament books.

In this series, we have invited some of the top Messianic Jewish theologians in the world to contribute their knowledge and understanding. Each has written on a book (or more) of the New Testament they've specialized in, making sure to present the Jewish aspects—the original context—of each book. These works are not meant to be a verse-by-verse exegetical commentary. There are already many excellent ones available. But, these commentaries supplement what others lack, by virtue of the fact they were not focusing on the Jewish aspects.

A number of different authors wrote these commentaries, each in his own style. Just as the Gospels were written by four different men, each with his own perspective and style, these volumes, too, have variations. We didn't want the writers to have to conform too much to any particular style guide, other than our basic one.

You may see some use the Hebrew transliteration of the names in the New Testament. Thus, one writer might refer to the Apostle to the Gentiles as Paul. Another might write,

Shaul, Paul's Hebrew name. Still, another might write Saul, an Anglicized version of Shaul. And some might write

Saul/Paul, to reject the different ways this servant of Messiah was known.

Another variation is the amount of reference material. Some have ample footnotes or endnotes, while others incorporate references within the text. Some don't have an enormous amounts of notes, based on the book they are writing commentary for.

We have plans for a Messianic Jewish commentary series on the entire bible. Although much has been written on the books of the Hebrew Scriptures, and there have been some written by Messianic Jews, there hasn't been a full commentary series on the "Older" Testament. But, we hope to publish such a series in the near future.

So, I invite you to put on your Jewish glasses (if you're not Jewish) and take a look at the New Testament in a way that will truly open up new understanding for you, as you get to know the God of Israel and his Messiah better.

RABBI BARRY RUBIN
Publisher
General Editor

BOOKS IN THE MESSIANIC COMMENTARY SERIES

MATTHEW PRESENTS YESHUA, KING MESSIAH

JAMES THE JUST PRESENTS APPLICATIONS OF TORAH

JUDE ON FAITH AND THE
DESTRUCTIVE INFLUENCE OF HERESY

RAV SHA'UL'S EXHORTATION TO THE
EPHESIANS ON JEWISH-GENTILE RELATIONS

FOREWORD

I n 1977, when I began working on my *Messianic Jewish Manifesto* (published in 1988 and in 1998 retitled *Messianic Judaism: A Modern Movement with an Ancient Past*), I wrote, "If I had a hundred Messianic Jewish scholars at my disposal, I could keep them all busy researching and writing till I reach the 120 years of age that everyone wishes me on my birthday." I said that among the books I would have them write were commentaries on books of the New Testament. Now people like Joshua Brumbach have come alongside and taken up the challenge in this Messianic commentary series.

Not only that, but Joshua represents the younger generation of Messianic Jews, and as an older-generation Messianic Jew I welcome his contributions and those of his contemporaries, who are expressing the life of the Messiah Yeshua in new ways.

His commentary on Jude is not a lengthy book, but the book of Jude is itself brief – which is why it easily gets lost in the shuffle. But because Joshua sees this book in the broad context of what Second Temple Judaism was, he can appreciate it as a weightier book than it would at first appear to be. He also sees the writer Jude as having a pastor's concern for his readers, wishing to protect them from being despoiled by people who would impose on them agendas other than the Messiah Yeshua's agenda. He also unpacks for us some of the lesser known and more intriguing things found in Jude – such as the reality of angels, the book of Enoch, and the allusion to the unknown burial place of Moses.

Let Joshua introduce you to the least noticed and least understood of New Covenant writers. You won't be disappointed!

DR. DAVID H. STERN
Author and Translator
Jerusalem, Israel

Author's Preface

Almost no other canonical book has been as neglected and overlooked as the Epistle of Jude. Why would such a little book, especially one said to be written by one of Yeshua's[1] own brothers, be so ignored? There are many possible reasons for this. Some consider it too controversial, difficult to follow, containing archaic imagery and taboo subjects better left alone.

Jude's letter challenges theological paradigms, raises questions about biblical authority, and confronts sexual misconduct. There are also those who find topics such as humans having sex with angels just too scandalous for the Bible.

But, this little book deserves far more attention than it currently receives. Jude packs an intellectual wallop! It may be small, but it has a big message that is just as relevant today as when it was originally written.

Jude offers us a rare glimpse into the earliest circles of Yeshua-followers when Yeshua's own blood relatives were still influential leaders and the movement's adherents were

---

1. The earliest followers of Jesus knew him by his original Hebrew name, Yeshua (ישוע), the masculine form of the word for Salvation/Redemption, (ישועה). In an attempt to more accurately portray the historical Jesus, and emphasize the Jewish context out of which he emerged, the name Yeshua will primarily be used.

still primarily Jewish. It reveals the issues and concerns that Yeshua's earliest Jewish followers wrestled with. In Jude's case, false teachers had appeared in some of the congregations, saying that the spiritual freedom they now have in Messiah gives them license to sin without consequence (v. 4). Jude thought this was a dangerous idea and wrote his letter as a vigorous rebuttal.

The letter is a warning to be on guard against dangerous people within the body of Messiah, particularly leaders who subtly violate their positions, making heretical ideas fashionable. Although appearing sound, such individuals do not have the best interests of the people in mind. Just as today, religious scandals and spiritual corruption were commonplace in Jude's world. His letter is a reminder to be careful and use sound judgment in choosing leaders.

Jude's letter also provides a portrait of a loving and devoted spiritual leader who is outraged by false teachers within the community. Jude addresses them head-on, exposing their spiritual and sexual corruption, while helping to guide believers toward the truth.

It is my hope that you will be inspired to delve into the world of Jude along with me as we explore its denunciation of false teachers, its *midrashic*[2] imagery and allusions - often drawn from apocryphal sources - and its challenge to remain faithful in a difficult world.

---

2. Midrash is an interpretive method and a creative body of literature that seeks to fill-in the gaps and answer questions within Scripture. It does so through delving into the deeper meaning of words, finding similarities with other biblical passages, and using Hebrew word plays, numerology and parables. Although Judah's letter is midrashic in style it is also important to note that it does not completely fit into the common understanding of the term Midrash as it is commonly used and understood.

This book will explore Jude in three parts. The first part will be a contextual introduction that provides a basic framework and background for understanding the second part, which is a running commentary on the entire text. Since Jude is such a short book, I have quoted it in its entirety, commenting in greater depth on particular verses and passages. In the conclusion, we will discuss the relevance of the Book of Judah today and it's personal application in the lives of believers. The appendix includes reflection questions which can be used for both individual and small group studies of the Book of Jude. Lastly, I have included a helpful glossary for certain words, references and concepts.

So let our journey into Jude begin!

PART ONE:
BACKGROUND

The Book of Jude is unusual. Far more than a simple treatise, it is a letter that the author never intended to write, and yet eventually considered important (v. 3). It is the product of "popular Judaism," reflecting the interests of the common people rather than the religious elite, which the author shares along with his readers.[3] It is also steeped in contemporary Jewish literature and tradition, drawing heavily upon Jewish apocalyptic ideas of Jewish understanding of morality (v. 5-7)". The letter was not haphazardly written, but carefully crafted, employing ancient literary and oratorical forms. The Book of Jude emphasizes continuity with the historical past, and yet modifies scriptural traditions and interpretations to achieve a particular purpose.[4] Therefore, we must delve into its underlying contexts and issues, and understand the Jewish world in which it was written.

---

3. Craig S. Keener, *The IVP Bible Background Commentary: New Testament* (Downers Grove: IVP Academic, 1993), 752.
4. Steven J. Kraftchick, *Jude, 2 Peter* (Abingdon New Testament Commentaries, Nashville: Abingdon Press, 2002), 17.

Who was Jude?

In the opening verse, the author describes himself as Jude. However, we should quickly note, as N.T. Wright does,[5] that the name is more accurately transliterated as Judah, from the Greek Ιουδαε *(Ieudah)* or Ιουδας *(Ieudas)*. The Greek corresponds with the original Hebrew יהודה *(Yehudah)*, which was and remains a common Jewish name.

Wright observes:

> It's interesting, isn't it, that we tend to call him "Jude," thereby distinguishing him from two others who had the same name: Judah the patriarch, the ancestor of Jesus, and Judas Iscariot. Why have we done that? He has a royal and ancient name, and I prefer that he should keep it.[6]

I do too. Although I have used the traditional name in the title and preface, in an attempt to be more historically and contextually accurate, I will primarily use the name Judah throughout the rest of this work, except where quoting other sources.

Who was Judah? The author simply describes himself as *"a servant[7] of Yeshua the Messiah and a brother of James (1:1)."* It has been traditionally understood that the James who is referred to here is James (i.e. *Ya'akov*) the brother of Yeshua, a leader within the fledging Yeshua-movement and a

---

5. N.T. Wright, *1 & 2 Peter and Jude* (N.T. Wright for Everyone Bible Study Guides, Downers Grove: Intervarsity Press, 2012), 6.

6. Ibid., 6.

7. Although Stern translated δουλος as "slave," I have opted here for "servant," in line with many other translations and scholarship.

sort of *nasi*,[8] the leader of the Jerusalem Council.[9] James also authored a letter in the New Testament bearing his name. As such, Judah would not only be a brother of James, but also of Yeshua. Ordinarily a person in Judah's time would describe himself as someone's son, rather than as someone's brother. The reason for the exception here seems to be James' prominence in the early Yeshua-following community in Jerusalem.

If Judah is in fact a brother of Yeshua, why doesn't he just come right out and say it? It is possible that he was just being humble. However, it is more likely that he did not feel the need to emphasize it. Although neither Judah nor James describe themselves as brothers of the Messiah, others did not hesitate to speak of them in this way (see Matt. 13:55; John 7:3-10; Acts 1:14; 1 Cor. 9:5; Gal. 1:19).[10]

Historically, most scholars have argued "almost certainly" that Judah was written by the actual brother of Yeshua.[11] However, there have also been challenges to this notion. One particular difficulty in attributing the letter to Judah is the language, since it is written with an impressive command of Greek, something that some consider unlikely for a poor Jew from the Galilee. According to Steven J. Kraftchick:

---

8. The term "*nasi*" is used regularly throughout the Hebrew Bible and often translated as "prince" or "captain." During the Second Temple period (c. 530 BCE – 70 CE) the term was also used for the highest ranking member of the Sanhedrin (the great assembly of sages).

9. The Council of Jerusalem was an early guiding body convened around 50/51 CE made up of the Apostles (Emmisaries), Elders, and other prominent figures within the Yeshua-believing community. For additional information see "Jerusalem Council" in the Glossary.

10. Burdick and Skilton, *op. cit.,* 1918.

11. Richard J. Bauckham, *Jude, 2 Peter* (World Biblical Commentary 50, Waco: Word Books, 1983), 14.

The author's command of literary Greek, a trait more likely to be found among Hellenistic Jews than among those of Palestinian origin, weighs against [Judah's authorship]. Thus, while it cannot be ruled out entirely, it is unlikely that Jude, the brother of James and Jesus, authored this letter.[12]

Kraftchick and other scholars argue that although the book is supposed to be written in the name of Judah, it was actually authored pseudepigraphically,[13] a common practice during the Second Temple period. If this is truly the case, why the author chose this particular pseudonym is not entirely clear. The best suggestion is that he chose the name because of Judah's connection with the early leaders of the community and the authority that would have implied.[14]

Recently, however, the position of Judah as being the actual author "has been defended with a whole series of new arguments."[15] For example, Richard Bauckham contends:

Although the author was certainly a Semitic speaker, who habitually used the Old Testament in Hebrew and probably the book of Enoch in Aramaic ... he also had a considerable command of good Greek. It is true that many recent studies have shown that both the Greek language and Hellenistic culture had penetrated

---

12. Kraftchick, *op. cit.,* 20-21.

13. Pseudepigraphic literature is a collection of non-canonical writings which became popular especially between 200 BCE and 200 CE. They often claim to have been written by biblical figures and prophets, but were actually written by an anonymous author, and often at a much later time in history.

14. Kraftchick, *op. cit.,* 21.

15. Peter J. Tomson, *If This Be From Heaven...* (Sheffield: Sheffield Academic Press, 2001), 336.

Jewish Palestine to a much greater extent than used to be supposed, but it is still surprising that a Galilean villager should show such a high degree of competence in the Greek language. On the other hand, it must be admitted that our knowledge is insufficient to set limits on the competence which the brother of Jesus could have acquired. He was probably still a very young man when he became a … missionary, and if his missionary travels took him among strongly Hellenized Jews there is no reason why he should not have deliberately improved his command of Greek to increase his effectiveness as a preacher. A wide vocabulary, which Jude has, is easier to acquire than a skill of literary style, where Jude's competence is less remarkable. The kinds of skills he shows are the rhetorical skills which a Jewish preacher in Greek would need.[16]

Furthermore, regarding the possibility of pseudonymous authorship, it is more likely that Judah's failure to mention that he is a sibling of Yeshua suggests authenticity since he did not see fit to emphasize it.[17]

It is helpful that references to the letter or quotations from it are found at a very early date, for example, by Clement of Rome around 96 CE.[18] According to Peter H. Davids, "Jude was cited relatively early and included in the early canon lists."[19] The book also seems to have been quite popular[20] and

16. Bauckham, *op. cit.,* 15.

17. Ibid., 14.

18. Burdick and Skilton, *op. cit.,* 1918.

19. Peter H. Davids, "Jude," *Theological Interpretation of the New Testament.* Ed. Kevin J. Vanhoozer (Grand Rapids: Baker Academic, 2005), 229.

20. J. N. D. Kelly, *The Epistles of Peter and of Jude* (Black's New Testament Commentary Series, London: Adam & Charles Black, 1969), 223.

remarkable evidence suggests that by the end of the second century it was widely accepted as canonical.[21] It was accepted and considered authentic by Clement of Alexandria (155-215), Tertullian (150-222) and Origen (185-253); and was included in the Muratorian Canon (c. 170). It was also accepted by Athanasius (298-373) and by the Council of Carthage (397).

In speaking of Yeshua's family, we do know that he had brothers and sisters:

> *Isn't he the carpenter's son? Isn't his mother called Miryam? and his brothers Ya`akov, Yosef, Shimon and Y'hudah? And his sisters, aren't they all with us? So where does he get all this?* (Matthew 13:55-56)

There were four brothers: Jacob (James/Ya'akov), who was the oldest, Joseph (Yosef), Shimon (Simon), and Judah (Jude/Y'hudah), who was the youngest of the brothers. No mention is made of his sisters' names. There were additional known descendants of Yeshua's family as well. This fact could provide additional support for Judah's authorship of the epistle, as it seems Judah's influence extended beyond his own lifetime and into successive generations. Evidence confirming this is found in Eusebius' *Church History*, which reports an older tradition concerning the grandsons of Judah. As Bo Reicke describes:

> Because of their relationship to Jesus, they were revered as descendants of David, and the emperor Domitian [81-96 CE], fearful of the development of dynastic traditions inimical to the empire, summoned

---

21. Bauckham, *op. cit.,* 17.

them before him; when he discovered that the men were merely poor farmers and no threat to Rome, he let them go (Eus. *Hist. eccl.* Iii. 19:1-20:6).[22]

Judah was likely very young at the time of Yeshua's death and resurrection. A few observations lead to this conclusion: Miryam probably gave birth to Yeshua around the age of 12 to 14. Her husband Joseph is believed to have died sometime between twelve and thirty years later. At the time of Yeshua's death she had four living sons and at least two unnamed daughters. Accounting for the possibility of a miscarriage or two during their marriage, it is quite possible that Judah was the last of eight to ten children, and would have been a young boy or teenager at the time of Yeshua's crucifixion.

It seems that Yeshua had a complicated relationship with his immediate family during his earthly life and ministry. They apparently did not believe he really was the Messiah:[23]

So his brothers said to him, "Leave here and go into Judea so that your disciples can see the miracles you do; for no one who wants to become known acts in secret. If you're doing these things, show yourself to the world!" His brothers spoke this way because they had not put their trust in him. (John 7:3-5)

It was only following Yeshua's death and resurrection that they became believers and served as leaders within the community.

---

22. Bo Reicke, *The Epistles of James, Peter and Jude* (The Anchor Bible, New York: Doubleday, 1964), 190-191.

23. Some scholars also reference Matthew 12:46-50.

We also know that Yeshua's family was quite devout in their commitment to God and Jewish observance. There is now overwhelming scholarly consensus on the "Jewishness of Jesus" and the thoroughly Jewish world within which his parents raised him and his siblings.[24] This commitment to Judaism should also be understood to extend to Judah as well. He was a faithful Jewish follower of the Messiah who understood his Yeshua-faith within an entirely Jewish context. This is true for all of the earliest Jewish believers and is the context within which the New Testament must be read.

When Was Judah Written?

Most scholars maintain that the Book of Judah was written between 60 and 90 CE.[25] However, it could also have been written as early as the 50's. As Burdick and Skilton point out, "there is nothing in the letter that requires a date beyond the lifetime of Jude the brother of the Lord."[26] If actually written by Judah, the brother of Yeshua, then it must have been written in the latter part of his life, which would support Bauckham's argument that throughout the course of his ministry, he certainly could have become quite adept at the Greek language.

The epistle clearly belongs to the milieu of Jewish apocalyptic literature and combats teachers of antinomian libertinism.[27] This makes it highly unlikely that it could be

---

24. See further: Amy-Jill Levine, *The Misunderstood Jew* (New York: Harper Collins, 2006); David Flusser, *The Sage from Galilee* (Grand Rapids: Eerdmans Publishing, 2007); James Charlesworth, Ed. *Jesus' Jewishness* (New York: Crossroad, 1997); Geza Vermes, *Jesus the Jew* (Minneapolis: Fortress Press, 1981); etc.

25. See the glossary for a description of these terms.

26. Burdick and Skilton, *op. cit.,* 1918.

27. Bauckham, *op. cit.,* 13. The term antinomian libertinism is explained further in the upcoming section, *What is the General Purpose?*

dated later than the first century CE. The relationship of Judah's epistle to 2 Peter must also be considered. If 2 Peter is largely based on Judah (the position of most scholars), then, "it favors an earlier rather than a later date for Jude."[28]

Who Were the Intended Recipients?

There is disagreement among scholars as to the intended recipients of the letter. Some argue the letter was primarily written to Jewish believers. Others favor a primarily Gentile believing audience. And still others maintain it could have been addressed to a combination of the two. However, due to the content, style and underlying assumptions, it seems a Jewish audience was in fact his primary focus.

It is also difficult to determine where the letter was first circulated geographically. Asia Minor, Syria or even Egypt has been posited. Considering the epistle's concern with false teachers, antinomianism and immoral behavior, some have used this to argue for a predominantly Gentile audience, since they had a greater need for learning righteous behavior than the Jews, who already had the Torah in their lives.

Peter J. Tomson argues that the evidence supports a Jewish audience "somewhere in the Holy Land."[29] However, Bauckham argues for a Jewish audience living within a predominantly Gentile environment:

> It is natural to think of predominantly Jewish Christian churches, both because they evidently come within the area of Jude's pastoral concern and responsibility, and also because of the high degree of familiarity with

---

28. Ibid., 13.
29. Tomson, *op. cit.,* 339.

9

> Jewish literature and traditions which Jude's allusions presuppose … Nevertheless the antinomian problem finds its most plausible context in a church in a Gentile environment (as in Paul's Corinth, and the churches of the book of Revelation). A predominantly, but not exclusively, Jewish Christian community in a Gentile society seems to account best for what little we can gather about the recipients of Jude's letter.[30]

This argument for a predominantly Jewish audience within a Gentile society seems quite plausible, and is the growing consensus among a number of scholars. By the time of Yeshua, the majority of Jews already lived outside of Israel, much like today. Although Judea and its environs obviously served as the Jewish homeland, and Jerusalem its holy center, the majority of the population lived around the Mediterranean, with a continually growing presence in Mesopotamia and expansion into Europe.

These Jewish communities within predominantly Gentile environments faced challenges quite different from their counterparts in Israel. As a minority, Jews were always considered "other." Their strange clothing, kosher diets, worldview, monotheism, and strict moral code set them apart from those around them, and there were extreme pressures to assimilate and conform to the pagan world around them. Politically, Jews were mostly excluded from Roman citizenship, and later, were forced to pay a unique tax, the *Fiscus Iudaicus*, due to their refusal to participate in the Imperial cult.[31]

---

30. Bauckham, *op. cit.,* 16.

31. The Imperial cult identified Roman emperors as divinely sanctioned authorities, and along with its various expected rituals, was inseparable from the worship of Rome's official deities. Jews, and later Christians, found this idea offensive refused to participate in the veneration.

Economically, Jews were also marginalized because of their wider social and political status. Often as non-citizens, they were forced into indentured servitude or professions that were on the fringes of society. There were even instances of expulsion. Under the reign of Tiberius, Jews were conscripted into the army and the remainder expelled from Italy between 19-31 CE.[32] After being allowed to return, Jews were again expelled from Rome under Claudius in 49 CE.[33]

Another reason this letter could have been addressed to a primarily Jewish audience within a wider Gentile environment is due to the concern about which Judah writes, a similar concern affecting Jewish followers of Yeshua to the present day – a pressure many Messianic Jews feel to give up their commitments to a Jewish way of life and worship under the guise that faith in Yeshua has "freed us from such 'legalistic'" bonds. In the particular case of Judah's epistle, the heresy is not just teaching a departure from the commands of the Torah, but also a strict ethical and moral code. This position was something Judah found abhorrent and even dangerous.

What is the General Purpose?

The primary purpose of an epistle was to address a particular issue within a certain community or group of communities. Because many others found the letters beneficial as well, they began to circulate beyond their original audience(s) and over time became well known. Judah's letter is no different.

---

32. Elmer Truesdell Merrill, "The Expulsion of Jews from Rome under Tiberius." *Classical Philology*. Vol. 14, No. 4, (October 1919): 365. JSTOR. Accessed April 2, 2014.

33. *Jewish Encyclopedia*. "Rome." Accessed April 2, 2014 - http://www.jewishencyclopedia.com/articles/12816-rome#anchor2.

Although it was originally written with a specific audience and purpose in mind, it was also general enough to be found useful by others beyond its original intent.

Judah initially set out to write a letter about salvation (v.3). However, he ended up writing a letter of warning concerning immoral intruders within the body of Messiah. He felt compelled to warn his audience about the dangers these individuals introduced and the rippling effects it could have upon the entire body of Messiah.

Apparently, these false teachers were trying to convince Yeshua-believers that their salvation, which was a pure act of grace, gave them license to sin since their sins would no longer be held against them.[34] Such distorted views of "hyper-grace" are prevalent within believing communities to this day. For example, it is easy to believe that God no longer sees the sins of his children since we have already been made righteous through the atonement of Yeshua. All of our sins, past, present and future, have already been forgiven. When taken further, this "hyper-grace" can even extend into believing that believers do not need to confess their sins or be convicted about them because God already sees us as perfect in his sight. However, this teaching is dangerous because it distorts God's grace and forgiveness and removes accountability, making it all too easy to compromise since "our sins are already forgiven." Such distorted views crept into the believing community very early; Judah confronts it head-on.[35]

As far as Judah's opponents, all we really know about them is that they were a group of teachers who traveled around to different communities and began influencing

---

34. Burdick and Skilton, *op. cit.,* 1919.
35. Paul also addresses this issue, for example, Romans 6:1-2.

them. Everything else Judah tells us about them is related to their antinomianism.

Antinomianism comes from a Greek expression meaning *lawlessness*. It is both a theological and pejorative term for the teaching that followers of Yeshua are not obligated to obey laws relating to ethics or morality. The term was first used by Martin Luther during the Reformation against Roman Catholicism. Because it is largely a pejorative term, few, if any, would explicitly call themselves "antinomian," therefore, it is usually a charge leveled by one group against another. This view is the polar opposite of legalism, the notion that obedience to religious law is necessary for salvation. In this sense, both antinomianism and legalism are considered errant extremes.[36]

Judah is specifically responding to the dangers of this doctrine. For Judah, as well as for other New Testament authors, there is no law or teaching which replaces the Torah, its way of life, and a common Jewish understanding of ethics and morality. This is a distortion of who Yeshua really is and his relationship to the Torah. This lawless worldview, which originated within Gnosticism,[37] viewed the body as a prison for the soul. The only way for the soul to escape and be truly free was to overcome the body through either one of two ways: strict physical discipline and the denial of physical comforts and pleasures, or by indulging fully into a hedonistic lifestyle.[38] The latter is the position of the false teachers Judah is addressing.

Along with their rejection of moral authority, Judah's opponents indulge in immoral behavior, especially sexual

---

36. Theopedia, "Antinomianism." Accessed March 24, 2014 - http://www.theopedia.com/Antinomianism
37. See the Glossary for a detailed explanation.
38. A belief that pleasure and happiness is the most important purpose in life.

misconduct (see verses 6-8 and 10). As Bauckham points out, by doing so, "they may be deliberately flouting accepted standards of Jewish morality and conforming to the permissiveness of pagan society."[39]

The World of Judah: Genre and Historical Context

The book of Judah conforms to the style of ancient Jewish letters. It begins with an introduction and greeting, which was the formal and essential part of the ancient letter. However, the body of the letter resembles more of a sermon:

> It consists of a midrash on a series of scriptural references and texts (vv 5-19) and [an encouragement to remain faithful] (vv20-23). The work closes with a doxology (vv 24-25), a conclusion more appropriate to a homily than to a letter.[40]

Yet it is still a letter. It could even be regarded as an "epistolary sermon," which was intended for a specific congregation(s), and then delivered as a homily, since Judah was unable to present the address himself. Even if the letter does not tell us exactly who the intended audience was, as Bauckham notes, "the content of the work makes it clear that it is not a tract against heresy in general … but a message for a specific situation in which a specific group of false teachers were troubling a specific [congregation] or group of [congregations]."[41]

The epistle draws heavily on popular, late Second Temple Period cosmic narratives to shape its understanding of the moral order of the universe.[42] During this period, the Torah

---

39. Ibid. Bauckham, *op. cit.,* 11.
40. Ibid., 3.
41. Ibid., 3.
42. Andrew S. Jacobs, "The Letter of Jude," *The Jewish Annotated New Testament*, Ed. Amy-Jill Levine and Marc Zvi Brettler (New York: Oxford, 2011), 460.

was elaborated upon through creative narratives filling in the words and deeds of the patriarchs and great leaders (i.e. *Enoch, Jubilees*, etc.). We also find elaborate angelology and apocalyptic expectation. The prophetic language, angelic outlook and apocalyptic influence of this letter intimately link it to its first century Jewish roots.[43]

Apocalyptic literature is a genre of prophetic writing that developed in post-exilic Jewish culture, beginning around the third-century BCE. The apocalyptic literature of Judaism and Christianity embraces a considerable period, from the centuries following the Babylonian exile to the close of the Middle Ages. The term "Apocalypse" (Ἀποκάλυψις) is a Greek word meaning "revelation," an unveiling or unfolding of things previously hidden. As a genre, apocalyptic literature details the authors' visions of the end times as often revealed through a heavenly messenger or angel.

The purpose of apocalyptic literature is to inspire hope. This is why it is often referred to as "crisis literature" – writings produced during a time of crisis. Sometime the crisis was military or political oppression – as in the biblical books of Daniel or Revelation. Sometimes the crisis was theological, as in the apocryphal book of 4 Ezra. At other times it was a sense of alienation – as in the Qumran writings.[44] In some cases the circumstances can no longer be determined.[45]

However, it is important to note the incredible influence of apocalyptic thinking on the New Testament as a whole. As Mitchell G. Reddish observes:

---

43. Ibid., 460. Also see: Peter Enns, *Inspiration and Incarnation: Evangelicals and the Problem of the Old Testament* (Grand Rapids: Baker Academic, 2005).
44. Referring to the Dead Sea Scrolls. See the Glossary for more information.
45. Mitchell G. Reddish, Ed. *Apocalyptic Literature: A Reader* (Peabody: Hendrickson, 1990), 24.

The apocalyptic worldview is pervasive in the New Testament writings. The resurrection of Jesus is understood as an apocalyptic event. The title "Son of Man" that is applied to Jesus in the Gospels is an apocalyptic phrase. Jesus' parables are mostly about the kingdom of God, again an apocalyptic notion. Eschatological judgment, resurrection, future rewards and punishments, destruction of evil forces, conflict between good and evil, angels and demons – all of these ideas in the New Testament are derived from an apocalyptic understanding of reality.[46]

Judah draws heavily upon Jewish apocalyptic ideas and morality. This is especially true in his use and interpretation of apocryphal sources, which is discussed later in the Introduction. Judah interprets and applies his sources in ways that demonstrate apocalyptic influence.

Language and Style

The letter of Judah is written with a remarkable command of the Greek language.[47] Much of the literary style and careful craftsmanship is lost to the average English speaker who cannot read Greek. Judah's use of Greek is described as "lively and vigorous," and according to Bauckham, "the whole work gives evidence of careful composition … Single words, phrases, and images are chosen for the associations they carry, and scriptural allusions and catchword connections increase the depth of meaning."[48]

---

46. Ibid., 30.
47. This is often used, as we discussed above, as an argument by some scholars against Judah being the actual author.
48. Bauckham, *op. cit.,* 6.

Kraftchick notes, "Four stylistic devices integrate the argument: comparison and contrast, a calculated use of hyperbole, poetic chaining through repetition, and the use of triads and catchwords."[49] He adds that there are at least twenty sets of triads in this brief letter. "These range from the author's initial self-identification as 'Jude, servant of Jesus Christ, and brother of James' (v. 1), to the final doxology, which lauds the one who is 'before all time, now, and forever.'"[50]

> The triple formulations underscore the urgency of the letter, attempting to make the readers see and feel the magnitude of the danger in their midst. Their use lends depth and vividness to the author's argument, causing his positive statements about God and the community to stand in direct contrast with the negative portrait of the antagonists.[51]

Considering its brevity, the letter also includes a high number of *hapax legomena*[52] - fourteen words which are not found elsewhere in the New Testament.[53] Of these, only four occur in the Septuagint (LXX). Additionally, there are three more words which only occur in the book of 2 Peter, who, as will be discussed below, most likely borrowed them from Judah.

What this wide range demonstrates is that Judah apparently had the ability to vary his vocabulary and style. His expressions

---

49. Kraftchick, *op. cit.,* 18.
50. Ibid., 19.
51. Ibid., 19.
52. Refers to a word which only occurs once either in a single text, a particular collection of texts (like the Bible), or the written record of a language.
53. Bauckham, *op. cit.,* 6.

are drawn from good literary, even poetic Greek.[54] He also demonstrates a good command of Greek idiom. Although "Semitisms"[55] can be found, [they] are not very prominent, probably less common than in most Jewish Greek."[56] This may seem a little unusual for a Galilean Jew like Judah, however it is not entirely inconceivable.

Sources

Despite Judah's competence in Greek, the author's contextual and intellectual background is clearly in the literature of Second Temple Judaism. The letter is written in Jewish Greek, which means that although there are only a few Semitisms, there is still enough vocabulary and sentence structure borrowed from Hebrew and Aramaic to make the letter feel like the work of a Jewish person whose native language is Semitic. This is especially evident in the background sources referenced within the text.

Bauckham points out that although it is often assumed that Judah, like many of the other New Testament authors, used the Septuagint as his underlying source for Tanakh quotes, this is a mistake:

> Much more significant is the fact that at no point where he alludes to specific verses of the [Old Testament] does he echo the language of the [Septuagint] … evidence show conclusively that it was the Hebrew Bible with which Jude was really familiar. When he wished to allude to it he did not stop to find the Septuagint

---

54. Ibid., 6.
55. The use of certain vocabulary, style and/or syntax influenced by, or borrowed from Hebrew and Aramaic.
56. Bauckham, *op. cit.,* 6.

translation, but made his own translation, in terms appropriate to the context and style of his work.[57]

Not only is Judah familiar with the Hebrew Bible, his use of apocryphal works is at least as extensive as his use of the Tanakh. He demonstrates close familiarity with 1 Enoch in verse 6 and directly quotes from it in verses 14-15. He also likely employs the *Testament of Moses* in verse 9.

Although the letter itself is composed in Greek, Judah is clearly a Hebraic speaker familiar with Jewish textual tradition and works, and readily makes use of them in his appeal.

Role and Use of Apocryphal Literature

Often considered a controversial subject is Judah's use of apocryphal sources. He refers to the *Testament of Moses* and quotes directly from 1 Enoch. He also draws on extra-biblical imagery and concepts, such as the *Nephilim* (fallen angels).[58]

Before we can dig further into our discussion we must first clarify what we mean by biblical literature. The term is often used to refer to three types of related writings relevant to biblical studies, including:

1) Canonical Scripture
2) Apocrypha (often referred to as Deuterocanonical books)
3) Pseudepigrapha

Canonical Scripture[59] are those books that are considered the most authoritative regarding matters of faith, theology and doctrine.

---

57. Ibid., 7.
58. This concept will be further discussed in the commentary to verse 6.
59. The word "canon" comes from the Greek κανών, meaning "rule" or "measuring stick."

The Apocrypha, or Deuterocanonical books, are additions not considered canonical by Jews and Protestant Christians; however, are often included in the published scripture of Roman Catholic and Orthodox Christians. Great examples are the books of Maccabees, which provide the background and context for the festival of Hanukkah.[60] Although Jews and Protestant Christians do not consider the Apocrypha canonical, they are nonetheless extremely valuable.

The final category is the Pseudepigrapha, which refers to a genre of non-canonical writings which became especially popular between 200 BCE and 200 CE. This body of literature claims to have been written by biblical figures and prophets, but was actually written by anonymous authors, and often at a much later time in history than the ascribed figures lived. Two examples are the works referenced in Judah - the *Testament of Moses* and *1 Enoch* (see the commentary to verses 9-10 and 14-16).

The troubling question for some is why Judah even quotes from these sources at all. It is important to acknowledge that the earliest followers of Yeshua shared a common Jewish theology and worldview of their time. Furthermore, the Hebrew Scriptures were not the only texts that influenced the writers of the New Testament. An excellent example of this is the concept of Melchizedek as described within the Book of Hebrews. The concept of Melchizedek as a lofty figure did not emerge directly from the Tanakh, where he is only mentioned twice (Genesis 14 and Psalm 110). Rather, the writer of Hebrews draws from an apocryphal tradition that had developed during

---

60. Hanukkah is also relevant to Christians, as it is referenced in the Gospel of John 10:22-39.

the Second Temple Period, which understood him to be a sort of mystical agent of God.[61] If one only considers the Hebrew Scriptures, then the Melchizedek described in Hebrews is a bit of a reach. But the portrait makes much more sense once this broader context is understood.[62]

We must remember that, chronologically, the Gospels do not immediately pick up where the Tanakh left off. The Second Temple period, which some scholars have labeled the "intertestamental period," was a time of incredible diversity and creativity. The Jewish world was very pluralistic and Jews interpreted and interacted with their scriptures differently than today.

And as noted above, diverse thought and imagery permeated Judaism at the time, and this includes the Judaism of the earliest followers of Yeshua. In order to make sense of the New Testament and its message, we need to go back and explore the period in which it was written and the sources upon which it draws.

Although we may not consider such pseudepigraphic sources authoritative today, at the time the New Testament was being written there was no set canon, and at various times these texts were considered authoritative by one group or another. Therefore, these apocryphal sources are extremely important to study for contextual background. Not just for the New Testament, but for what Judaism was like before the birth of what would eventually become Rabbinic Judaism and

---

61. This is especially true when one looks at extant literature from the Second Temple period, and particularly 11QMelch within the Dead Sea Scrolls.

62. By making such a statement, I am certainly not claiming that Hebrews is unreliable. I am simply pointing out the historical context out of which Hebrews emerged.

21

Christianity, two siblings which both emerged together out of Second Temple Judaism.[63]

Relationship to 2 Peter

The similarities between 2 Peter (especially chapter two) and the Epistle of Judah are quite remarkable. Like Judah, 2 Peter has also largely been an ignored book, for many of the same reasons. Both books demonstrate incredible concern regarding immoral intruders within the body of Messiah:

> *But among the people there were also false prophets, just as there will be false teachers among you. Under false pretenses they will introduce destructive heresies, even denying the Master who bought them, and thus bring on themselves swift destruction. Many will follow their debaucheries; and because of them, the true Way will be maligned. In their greed they will exploit you with fabricated stories. Their punishment, decreed long ago, is not idle; their destruction is not asleep!* (2 Peter 2:1-3)

J. N. D. Kelly observes, "The close relationship between the two epistles is evident from their startling resemblances in subject-matter, vocabulary and phrasing, and even order of ideas."[64] Many have argued that these numerous similarities are no coincidence. According to Peter H. Davids, "the interpretation

---

63. According to Gabriele Boccaccini, "Scholars now place Rabbinic Judaism and Christianity on the same level as legitimate heirs of ancient Judaism. Christianity and Judaism grew out of the same soil and were formed at the same time ... The two are more like 'fraternal twins,' born of the same womb." ("Multiple Judaisms," *Bible Review*, Vol. XI, Num. I, February 1995, 41)

64. Kelly, *op. cit.,* 225.

of Jude begins with 2 Peter, who edits and adapts Jude, such as removing the direct references to the Pseudepigrapha, to form his second chapter."[65] Kraftchick writes:

> While there is almost no example of identical wording in Jude and 2 Peter, the linguistic correspondence between them are too numerous to be explained by coincidence … The connections between Jude 4-16 and 2 Peter 2:1-18 are unmistakable, and only some form of literary dependence can explain the high degree of overlap.[66]

The following table illustrates the parallel passages:[67]

Jude	2 Peter
4	2:1-2
5	2:3
6	2:4
7	2:6
8	2:10
9	2:11
10	2:12
11	2:13-16
12	2:13, 17
13	2:17
16	2:18
17	3:1-2
18	3:3

---

65. Davids, *op. cit.,* 229.
66. Kraftchick, *op. cit.,* 79.
67. Ibid., 79.

Due to literary and linguistic similarities between the books, the majority of scholars believe that Judah was in fact written first, and that 2 Peter shows signs of literary dependence on the earlier work.[68] They are both concerned with false teachers, they both draw upon the same passages from the Hebrew Bible; and both draw on similar apocryphal imagery, including references to the fallen angels. However, as Kraftchick points out, although "Jude served as a source for 2 Peter, the author added, edited, and, on occasion, omitted material from the letter as his own argument required."[69]

Canonical Order: Why is Jude (almost) Last?

Another critical issue we must consider is what role the order of the books in the New Testament plays in our conception of Judah. In our current order of the canon, Judah is stuck all the way in the back, just before Revelation – almost as an afterthought. But what if Judah was not in the back, but rather placed toward the front - after the Gospels and before Paul's letters? Would it then change how we read it? Would we maybe perceive it as more relevant and important if it were closer to the front?

In actuality, this may originally have been the case. In the three oldest canonical orders of the New Testament, from codices *Vaticanus, Sinaiticus and Alexandrinus*, two of them place the "General Epistles," which include Judah, after the Gospels and Acts:[70]

---

68. Bauckham, *op. cit.*, xii.
69. Kraftchick, *op. cit.*, 80.
70. The below chart: John W. Miller, *How the Bible Came to Be* (New York: Paulist Press, 2004), 57 *(emphases and dates mine)*.

Codex Vaticanus	**Codex Sinaiticus**	**Codex Alexandrinus**
(c. 4th century)	*(c. mid-4th century)*	*(c. 5th century)*
Matthew	Matthew	Matthew (25:6-28:20 only)
Mark	Mark	Mark
Luke	Luke	Luke
John missing)	John	John (6:50-8:52
Acts	Romans	Acts
James	1 Corinthians	James
1 Peter	2 Corinthians	1 Peter
2 Peter	Galatians	2 Peter
1 John	Ephesians	1 John
2 John	Philippians	2 John
3 John	Colossians	3 John
JUDE	1 Thessalonians	**JUDE**
Romans	2 Thessalonians	Romans
1 Corinthians	Hebrews	1 Corinthians
2 Corinthians	1 Timothy	2 Corinthians (4:13-12:6 missing)
Galatians	2 Timothy	Galatians
Ephesians	Titus	Ephesians
Philippians	Philemon	Philippians
Colossians		Colossians
1 Thessalonians	Acts	1 Thessalonians
2 Thessalonians	James	2 Thessalonians
Hebrews (1:1-9:14)	1 Peter	Hebrews
	2 Peter	1 Timothy
(Ending lost,	1 John	2 Timothy
including the	2 John	Titus
Pastorals)	3 John	Philemon
	JUDE	Revelation
	Revelation	1 Clement (2-12:5)
	Barnabas	
	Shepherd of Hermas	

This observation has tremendous implications for how we read Judah. The books were placed in a specific order to highlight a particular narrative structure. This is one reason why the Jewish and Christian canons of the Hebrew Scriptures differ. The books are the same, but were placed in different orders, thereby stressing different narrative arcs. In a canonical structure which places Judah much earlier in the order, greater prominence is placed on the book and its relation to all the others. It becomes a tool to thereby interpret the epistles which follow.

Maybe Judah was never intended to be so insignificant. Which leads us to ask ourselves, what if we considered Judah's letter as prominently as Paul's many letters? This would dramatically change the way we not only view Judah's epistle but could even alter the way we view other letters within the New Testament as well. However, to discover these implications, we must look further into the text itself.

Outline of the Book

1   Address and Greeting
3   Purpose of the Letter
       a. The Appeal *(v.3)*
       b. Reason for the change in subject *(v.4)*
5-16 *Midrash/Pesher* - Warning Against False Teachers
       a. Tanakh Types I
            i.   Unbelievers within Israel *(v.5)*
            ii.   *Nephilim* (Fallen Angels) *(v.6)*
            iii. Sodom and Gomorrah *(v.7)*
            iv. Interpretation/Application (v.7b-8)
       b. Michael and Satan (v.9)

PART TWO:
COMMENTARY

Address and Greeting (v. 1-2)

1 *From: Y'hudah, a slave of Yeshua the Messiah and a brother of Ya'akov.[71] To: Those who have been called, who are loved by God the Father and kept for Yeshua the Messiah:* **2** *May mercy, love and shalom be yours in full measure.*

The author identifies himself as Judah, from the Greek Ιουδαε *(Ieudah)* or Ιουδας *(Ieudas)*; corresponding to the original Hebrew יהודה *(Yehudah)*, a common name among the Jewish people. Of those in the New Testament with the same name, or a variation of it (Jude, Judas, Judah), the two most likely candidates for authorship are: 1) Judas the Apostle (Luke 6:16; Acts 1:13) – not to be confused with Judas Iscariot – and 2) Judah the brother of Yeshua (Mt. 13:55; Mark 6:3).[72]

As stated in the Introduction (see *"Who was Jude?"*), it is traditionally understood that the author was Judah the brother of Yeshua, and also of James. Although some scholars have questioned this and assumed pseudonymous authorship, after

---

71. Jacob (i.e. James)
72. Burdick and Skilton, *op. cit.,* 1918.

weighing the evidence, there is no good reason to dismiss Yeshua's youngest brother as the actual author.

The opening and greeting of the epistle "was the most stereotyped part of the ancient letter, and Jude here follows the form of the Jewish letter of his day."[73] Most of the early letters in the New Testament specify a "formula of destination," meaning they are addressed to a specific group or community. However, Judah's failure to do this has erroneously led many over the centuries to assume it was a general letter written to all of Yeshua's followers. Although the book contains instructions and guidance helpful for all believers, Judah originally intended for this letter to be sent to a specific audience and to address a particular issue.

Regarding the blessing in verse 2, *"May mercy, love and shalom be yours in full measure"* Kraftchick comments:

> Ancient Jewish letter writers used the phrase "mercy and peace" to express their desire that the divine blessing of *hesed* and *shalom* rest on the letter's recipients always and forever. Jude's formulation … bears a close resemblance to these Jewish blessings, but it adds the term "love" to their typical dyad.[74]

By adding the word "love," this addition also provides messianic overtones to the blessing and emphasizes a fundamental theme (vv. 1, 2, 3, 17, 20, 21), "the love of God," as a foundation for God's community, echoing a central concept of Yeshua's teachings and the entire New Testament.

---

73. Bauckham, *op. cit.,* 19.
74. Kraftchick, *op. cit.,* 28.

Purpose of the Letter (v. 3-4)

3 Dear friends, I was busily at work writing to you about the salvation we share, when I found it necessary to write, urging you to keep contending earnestly for the faith which was once and for all passed on to God's people. 4 For certain individuals, the ones written about long ago as being meant for this condemnation, have wormed their way in - ungodly people who pervert God's grace into a license for debauchery and disown our only Master and Lord, Yeshua the Messiah.

The Appeal (v. 3)

Judah initially set out to write an epistle concerning "*the salvation we share.*" However, he found it necessary to write a letter urging his audience "*to keep contending earnestly for the faith which was once and for all passed on to God's people.*" He was concerned that they were being influenced and could possibly be waning in their faith. So Judah urges them to stay strong and faithful. The reason for this concern is then addressed in verse 4.

The opening word in v.3, Ἀγαπητοί (*agapētoi*), which is often, translated "Beloved," and by David H. Stern simply as "friends," was a common greeting among the early followers of Yeshua. At the end of verse 3 Judah also employs the term ἁγίοις (*hagiois*), usually translated as "saints," and more correctly by Stern as "God's people," which was a phrase readily familiar to Judah's Jewish audience. By "God's people," Judah not only means the covenant-elect people of Israel, but also a greater extension of Israel reflected in Ephesians 2, Romans 11 and Acts 15, etc. Through faith in Yeshua, Gentiles are now miraculously included within the commonwealth of Israel -

31

not by displacing the Jewish people or through conversion to Judaism, but rather simply through faith in Israel's Messiah. This is why Judah discusses *"the salvation we share."* As Kelly notes, "It brings out the corporate nature of salvation as understood by Judaism, with its consciousness of being the people of God."[75]

Stern comments, "[Verse 3], along with v. 17 … suggests that the letter was written in the latter part of the first century when 'the faith' had begun to crystalize. This use of Greek *pistis* to mean a systematized body of doctrine is unusual … but even here we should not limit 'the faith' to its intellectual aspects; it includes and implies not only doctrine to be believed, but the entire Messianic way of life to be observed."[76]

Judah is concerned with more than just the proper theology and doctrine of these believers; he is concerned with the entirety of their spiritual lives, including their behavior. From a Jewish perspective, our thoughts and actions are intimately linked and must not only be consistent, but a natural outgrowth of the other. Judaism is not as concerned with correct theology as much as it is with one's behavior, because behavior is a reflection and the proof of our thinking and relationship with God. As the old adage goes, "actions speak louder than words." Therefore deviations of faith are also a dilemma of ethics. As Peter H. Davids observes, "ethical deviations are deviations from the faith as much as or more than doctrinal deviations, and that eschatological expectation determines and enforces ethics."[77]

---

75. Kelly, *op. cit.,* 246.
76. David H. Stern. *Jewish New Testament Commentary* (Clarksville: Jewish New Testament Publications, 1992).
77. Davids, *op. cit.,* 231.

The earliest followers of Yeshua felt a profound obligation to live and act in a way that hastened the return of the Messiah. Their conviction poses a challenge to us today to live, act, and think in the same way. We must live with an understanding that the true fruit of our relationship with God is determined by how we live it out through our deeds.[78]

The Reason for the change in subject (v. 4)

Immoral "intruders," or false teachers, penetrated the community of believers and, according to Judah, no longer recognized Yeshua's right to command obedience. They began teaching that a person is considered righteous by God regardless of their moral life and behavior. However, as discussed in the Introduction (see *What is the General Purpose?*), such distorted views of "hyper-grace" persist even into this present day. For example, there are those who teach that because we have already been forgiven through Yeshua's atonement, we do not need to confess our sins or be convicted about them because God already sees us as perfect in his sight. But this teaching is dangerous because it distorts God's grace and forgiveness and removes accountability, making it all too easy to compromise.

With the phrase, *"the ones written about long ago,"* Judah now begins his exegesis of the Tanakh and apocryphal texts to demonstrate that this false teaching is so dangerous and heretical that Scripture already warned of them "long ago." Although the original context of those texts is entirely different, through a creative literary method, he begins to apply and interpret these verses to refer to these specific false teachers.

---

78. James 1:22-27, 2:14-18, 2:21-26 and Matthew 7:16-20.

Midrash/Pesher (v. 5-16)

Tanakh Types – First Set Of Three (v. 5-8)

5 *Since you already know all this, my purpose is only to remind you that the Lord, who once delivered the people from Egypt, later destroyed those who did not believe.* **6** *And the angels that did not keep within their original authority, but abandoned their proper sphere, he has kept in darkness, bound with everlasting chains for the Judgment of the Great Day.***7** *And Sodom, Gomorrah and the surrounding cities, following a pattern like theirs, committing sexual sins and perversions, lie exposed as a warning of the everlasting fire awaiting those who must undergo punishment.* **8** *Likewise, these people, with their visions, defile their own flesh, despise godly authority and insult angelic beings.*

Judah now begins his *midrashic*[79] interpretation (verses 5-16) of fallen characters in the Tanakh and various apocryphal texts, and directly applies it to the false teachers of his time. The New Testament writers believed they were living in the "End Times" and interpreted their Scriptures through this interpretive lens. According to Bauckham:

> Jude's midrashic method bears some comparison with the pesher exegesis in Qumran. There is the same conviction that the ancient texts are eschatological prophecy which the interpreter applies to the events of his own time, understood as the time of eschatological

---

79. Although Judah's letter is midrashic in style, it is also important to note that it does not completely fit into the common understanding of the term Midrash as it is commonly used and understood. See the Glossary for more information on this term.

fulfillment. Whereas the main Qumran pesharim are commentaries on whole passages or whole books of the [Old Testament] ("continuous pesharim"), there are also "thematic pesharim" ... which are commentaries on a collection of texts on one theme, in this resembling Jude's midrash.[80]

There are, however, important differences between Judah and the *pesharim* of the Dead Sea Scrolls. The Qumran pesharim offer no analogies for Judah's quotation of apocryphal books (vv. 9, 14-15), his quotes of apostolic prophecies (vv.17-18), or his abbreviation of Scriptures instead of actual quotations from the Tanakh (vv. 5-7, 11). Furthermore, Judah's particular use of typology is also not found in the Qumran pesharim.[81]

Regarding this first set of three "Tanakh types" (*Unbelievers within Israel, the Nephilim,* and *Sodom and Gomorrah),* Kraftchick comments:

This section introduces a series of examples that demonstrates the consequences of opposing God's actions and designs. Jude presents three events, each of which contains three distinctive facets: (1) a relationship with God is established, (2) those given this status refuse to accept it and oppose the will or purpose of God, and (3) this disobedience results in divine judgment. Jude's primary focus in these examples is not the wrath of God; rather, the focus is on the rejection by those who have received God's responsibilities that their favored status entails.[82]

---

80. Bauckham, *op. cit.,* 5.
81. Ibid., 5.
82. Kraftchick, *op. cit.,* 35-36.

Judah is drawing upon a traditional schema within the ancient world where these three examples were commonly listed together. The main context of this traditional arrangement was to encourage its hearers not to follow these examples.[83] That is why Judah's letter begins by "reminding" his readers of these things. The command to "remind" and "remember" (rooted in the Hebrew concept of זכור, *zachor* throughout the Bible)[84] is grounded in God's acts in history, and Jewish writers often urged their readers to "remember" these redemptive acts.

This idea of remembering is actually a command to do "this" because God did "that." It is not just a recollection, but an embracing of our covenantal obligations. According to Brevard Childs, "Memory plays a central role in making Israel constantly aware of the nature of God's benevolent acts as well as her own covenantal pledge."[85] Therefore, when Israel is told to *"remember the Sabbath day, to keep it holy* (Exodus 20:8),*"* or when Yeshua tells his disciples *"do this in remembrance of me* (Luke 22:19, 1 Cor. 11:2:4),*"* this remembrance is a covenantal act.

Example One: Unbelievers within Israel (v. 5)

We must first establish that *"unbelievers within Israel"* is not a general reference to Israel as whole, or to Israel's covenant election, but to specific individuals within that redeemed community.

83. Bauckham, *op. cit.,* 46.

84. Its Greek equivalent found in the Septuagint and New Testament is ἀνάμνησις (*anamnesis).*

85. Brevard S. Childs, *Memory and Tradition in Israel* (London: SCM Press, 1962), 51.

The specific phrase, *"later destroyed those who did not believe"* refers to the account of Numbers 14, where the people of Israel were discouraged by the report of the spies who returned from Canaan and grumbled against Moses and Aaron, and demonstrated a complete lack of faith in God's promises. As a result of their unbelief, God ruled that the entire generation over the age of twenty (except Joshua and Caleb) would perish in the wilderness and not enter the Promised Land.[86]

There is another discussion related to who *"delivered the people from Egypt."* The majority of scholars agree that the authoritative translation is the one which reads that it was the LORD who delivered Israel. However, other early manuscripts read that it was Yeshua who redeemed Israel from Egypt: *"Now I want to remind you, although you once fully knew it, that Jesus, who saved a people out of the land of Egypt ...* (ESV)."[87]

Most of the manuscripts read *"kyrios* (κύριος)," the Lord. However, there are other early important attestations to *"Iésous* ('Ιησοῦς)," Jesus/Yeshua. Although this might seem trivial (and redundant) to some, we must ask, which is it? The LORD[88] or Yeshua?

Kraftchick proposes:

> Jude's Jewish source material clearly contained the word "Lord" *(kyrios)* as a title for God. But three factors intended his readers to understand it as a reference to Christ. First, Jude makes this substitution in verse 14. Second, he has just referred to "Lord Jesus Christ" in verse 4, and three other times he explicitly connects

---

86. Ibid., 49.
87. *The Holy Bible: English Standard Version* (Wheaton: Crossway, 2002), 1027.
88. i.e. Specifically יהוה, "HaShem/Adonai" or "God the Father"

Jesus Christ with the title "Lord" (v.17, 21, 25). Third, the New Testament includes other references to the activity of the pre-existent Christ (e.g. 1 Cor 10:4, 9; Phil 2:6).[89]

Bauckham believes that the use of this typology was not originally intended by Judah. Although in the early centuries the similarities, both linguistically and typologically, between Joshua ben Nun *(Yehoshua)* and Jesus *(Yeshua)* were frequently exploited in the interests of similar typology, it is argued that, instead of Judah, this typology could have been attractive to a later scribe who changed *kyrios* to *Iésous*.[90] However, according to Kelly and others, the rendering which reads that it was the LORD who delivered His people "almost certainly is the true text."[91]

Example Two: Nephilim (Fallen Angels) (v. 6)

Judah writes, *"And the angels that did not keep within their original authority, but abandoned their proper sphere, he has kept in darkness, bound with everlasting chains for the Judgment of the Great Day."*

Another controversial topic is the *Nephilim*, fallen angels. Judah not only uses them as an example of arrogance and rebellion, but alludes to an expanded tradition common during the Second Temple period, that the *Nephilim* cohabited with human women creating a hybrid race of "giants" (see Gen. 6:1-4). This is best exemplified in the interpretation of this passage as found in 1 Enoch 6-19.

---

89. Kraftchick, *op. cit.,* 37.
90. Bauckham, *op. cit.,* 43.
91. Kelly, *op. cit.,* 254.

The Books of Enoch are a collection of writings attributed to the biblical figure Enoch (Gen. 5:18-24), but were actually composed by several anonymous authors. 1 Enoch, also known as *Ethiopic Apocalypse of Enoch*, is the oldest of the books bearing the name and dates between the second century BCE and the first century CE. Although fragments of the work have been discovered in Aramaic, Greek and Latin, it is found complete only in the Ethiopic (*Ge'ez*) version. 1 Enoch itself is "clearly composite, representing numerous periods and writers."[92]

Genesis 5:24 simply states, *"Enoch walked with God, and then he wasn't there, because God took him."* According to E. Isaac, "This tradition of Enoch's spiritual relocation gave rise to many haggadic stories, including one that …when he was taken away by God, he saw the secrets of the mysteries of the universe, the future of the world, and the predetermined course of human history."[93]

1 Enoch was well known within early Jewish circles, particularly among the Essenes, as well as the early Yeshua-followers. It was referenced in other pseudepigraphic works and Isaac points out:

> Some New Testament authors seem to have been acquainted with the work, and were influenced by it, including Jude, who quotes it explicitly (1:14-15). At any rate, it is clear that Enochic concepts are found in various New Testament books, including the Gospels and Revelation."[94]

---

92. E. Isaac. "1 (Ethiopic Apocalypse of) Enoch," *The Old Testament Pseudepigrapha*, Ed. James H. Charlesworth. (Peabody: Hendrickson, 1983), 5.
93. Ibid., 5.
94. Ibid., 8.

Recounting this belief about the *nephilim*, the Jewish historian Josephus wrote, "Many angels accompanied with women, and begat sons that proved unjust" (*Antiquities* 1:73).[95]

Based on this interpretative tradition, which was common in the first century, in the primordial period before Noah's flood, 200 angels rebelled against God, forsook their place in heaven and descended upon the earth (1 Enoch 6:6). They took wives from among human women and had sexual relations with them (7:1), and taught many things to earth's inhabitants:

> And they [the *nephilim*] taught them magical medicine, incantations, the cutting of roots, and taught them (about) plants. And the women became pregnant and gave birth to great giants whose heights were three hundred cubits. These (giants) consumed the produce of all the people until the people detested feeding them. So the giants turned on (the people) in order to eat them. And they began to sin against the birds, wild beasts, reptiles, and fish. And their flesh was devoured the one by the other, and they drank blood (7:1-6).[96]

Another sin the *nephilim* committed was that they ate meat and consumed blood. Why is this viewed as a sin? Because according to the Torah itself (Genesis 1:29-30), all living creatures, both humans and animals, were to be vegetarian. It is not until after the flood that created beings were allowed to eat meat (Genesis 9:3-7).

---

95. William Whiston, *The Works of Josephus: Complete and Unabridged* (Peabody: Hendrickson, 1987), 32.
96. Isaac, *op. cit.,* 16.

Not only did these Fallen Angels lust after human women and have sexual relations with them, they supposedly also taught humans about things they were not ready for. According to 1 Enoch, the *nephilim* shared with humans their knowledge about weapons, jewelry and cosmetics (8:1-2), and concludes: "All their conduct became corrupt (8:2)."

According to 1 Enoch and this wider interpretive tradition, the *nephilim* and the sin they introduced to humanity was the primary reason for the flood. God flooded the earth to cleanse it from all its evil and corruption, and the offending angels were imprisoned in darkness (chapter 10).

Kelly maintains that these angels were given "dominion" or "authority," but did not keep within it. In the New Testament, he argues, they appear with such titles as "principalities" or "principalities and powers" (Rom. 8:38; Col. 2:15: the Greek for 'principality' is *archē*), or even "world rulers" (Eph. 6:12). The basis of this belief is that the nations of the world had been assigned to them (according to the Septuagint's reading of Deut. 32:8), and the whole course of the universe was placed under their supervision. Therefore, Kelly asserts, they had *"their proper sphere* (v.6)," which 1 Enoch (12:4 and 15:3, 7) calls "the high heaven, the holy eternal place." But those of their number who lusted after the daughters of men committed the sin of abandoning this heavenly dwelling-place by failing to keep within their proper authority.[97]

Because these angels abandoned their "proper authority," Judah writes, God *"has kept them in darkness, bound with everlasting chains for the Judgment of the Great Day."* The book of Genesis does not actually record this penalty, but it is

---

97. Kelly, *op. cit.,* 256-257.

again creatively expanded in full detail within 1 Enoch, which is clearly Judah's primary source:[98]

> Enoch, scribe of righteousness, go, and declare to the Watchers of heaven who have left their high heaven and, the holy eternal place, and have defiled themselves with women … They have defiled themselves with great defilement upon the earth; neither will there be peace unto them nor the forgiveness of sin … But they shall groan and beg forever over the destruction of their children, and there shall not be peace unto them forever … As for Enoch, he proceeded to Azaz'el [their leader], "There will not be peace unto you; a grave of judgment has come upon you." (1 Enoch 12:4-13:1)[99]

Example Three: Sodom and Gomorrah (v. 7)

In verse 7, Judah provides a third example of disobedience and judgment from the Tanakh, recalling the story of Sodom and Gomorrah (Genesis 19). According to Judah, the sin of Sodom and Gomorrah (and its surrounding cities) was the corruption and licentiousness of its inhabitants, especially their eagerness to have sexual relations with the two angels whom Lot was hosting. Both Bauckham and Kraftchick note that this story "had long been regarded as a paradigm case of divine judgment."[100]

By using this example, Judah is able to make a second connection between disobedience and sexual misconduct. Like the angels who engaged in illicit intercourse with women (1 Enoch 7:1), Sodom's inhabitants also pursued illicit relations.

---

98. Ibid., 257.
99. Isaac, *op. cit.,* 19.
100. Quote from Kraftchick, 39; cf. Bauckham, 53.

Judah highlights this disobedience with the phrase, *"following a pattern like theirs* [the fallen angels]*, committing sexual sins and perversions, lie exposed as a warning of the everlasting fire awaiting those who must undergo punishment"* (this was already alluded to in v. 4).

In this example, however, the roles of human and divine are reversed. In 1 Enoch the fallen angels sought sexual relations with humans, but in v. 7 it is the inhabitants of Sodom who seek to cohabit with the angels. Judah refers to this as "going after other flesh" (σαρκὸς ἑτέρας, *sarkos heteras*). The primary point here is not that the residents of the city sought to have sex with their male visitors, but that they sought relations with angelic beings of an entirely different order.[101]
Kelly comments:

> While the writer is singling out the Cities of the Plain as examples of immorality, his attention is focused not so much on their unnatural conduct (for this, cf. Rom. 1:24; 27) as on the close parallel between their behavior and that of the wicked angels. Both had made their sin even more appalling by lusting after "different flesh" - the angels because, spiritual beings though they were, they had coveted mortal women, and the Sodomites because, though only human beings, they had sought intercourse with angels.[102]

Interpretation/Application (v. 7b-8)

With these first three examples from the Tanakh *(Unbelievers within Israel, the Nephilim, and Sodom and Gomorrah)*,

---

101. Ibid., Kraftchick, 39.
102. Kelly, *op. cit.,* 6-7.

Judah illustrates the dire consequences of disobeying God and transgressing the perceived natural order of God's creation. That is why, Judah states, *"They serve as an example of those who suffer the punishment of fire* (v.7, *NIV*)." The reference here to fire is meant to allude to the final punishment reserved for both the inhabitants of Sodom and Gomorrah (Gen. 19:24) and the wicked angels (1 Enoch 10:13-14).

In verse 8 he calls these false teachers "dreamers," either because they claimed to receive visions or, more likely, because their passions were out of touch with the realities of holiness, and they perceived themselves as replacing the authority of the apostles and the Torah. Judah accuses the false teachers of rejecting divine authority, a charge initially alleged in v. 4. Kraftchick points out that these two verses thus frame the thought of the entire section. By echoing key words, "Jude creates a chain from the primordial disobedience of the angels and the immorality of Sodom to the behavior of the intruders."[103]

The Archangel Michael And Satan (v. 9-10)

9 *When Michael, one of the ruling angels, took issue with the Adversary, arguing over the body of Moshe, he did not dare bring against him an insulting charge, but said, "May ADONAI[104] rebuke you."* **10** *However, these people insult anything they don't understand; and what they do understand naturally, without thinking, like animals - by these things they are destroyed!*

---

103. Kraftchick, *op. cit.,* 41.

104. Literally, "My Lord," a Hebrew word used by Jews to represent the tetragrammaton, the sacred name of God consisting of the four Hebrew letters, *Yud-Hey-Vav-Hey*; but usually as LORD (all capital letters in many Bibles).

Judah here refers to a Jewish tradition where the archangel Michael and Satan *"took issue ... arguing over the body of Moshe."* Provoked to anger by Satan (who charged that Moses was a murderer and his body was not worth burying), Michael refrained from bringing *"an insulting charge"* against him.

This reference is believed to be drawn from *The Testament of Moses* (or *Assumption of Moses*), an incomplete apocryphal text composed sometime in the first-century CE but known in modern times from a poorly preserved Latin manuscript discovered by A. M. Ceriani in the Ambrosian Library of Milan, and published in 1861. Although there is only a single extant manuscript, the text was known from much earlier references in patristic literature and lists.[105] Our only existing copy is an incomplete text describing Moses' final words to Joshua just prior to his death and is believed to have recorded Moses' death and "burial"/taking of Moses' body to heaven,[106] which is referenced in Judah 9.

According to J. Priest:

> It was apparent to the first editors that the Latin was translated from Greek ... Further investigation, however, indicates that the Greek itself was, in all probability, a translation of a Semitic original. This view is almost universally accepted today, but there remains a question as to whether the original was Aramaic or Hebrew. Certainty is not possible, but the balance of probability leans toward Hebrew.[107]

---

105. The writings of early Christian leaders often referred to as the Church Fathers.
106. J. Priest. "Testament of Moses," *The Old Testament Pseudepigrapha*, Ed. James H. Charlesworth. (Peabody: Hendrickson, 1983), 919-920.
107. Ibid., 920.

This story as recorded in *The Testament of Moses* seems to be an allusion to an ancient tradition of stories in which Satan, as the accusing angel, and Michael, the chief of the angels and acting as the patron of God's people, engaged in legal disputes over Israel. This tradition supposedly goes back to Zechariah 3, the source of Judah's words *"May ADONAI rebuke you"* (3:2).

The story of Moses' burial in the *Testament of Moses* was one of a number of legends which grew up around the death and burial of Moses, stimulated by the account in Deuteronomy 34:1-6. The Torah's description of these events is quite vague. God forbade Moses from entering the Promised Land. However, he was granted the unique privilege of being buried by God himself in a grave unknown to any human being. In line with the general tendency of pseudepigraphic literature, the *Testament of Moses* ascribed the burial to Michael who acted as God's agent. After Moses' death atop Mt. Nebo, Michael was to retrieve the body and move it to another place and bury it. However, before he could do so, he encountered Satan who was intent on gaining control of the body. Therefore, Michael and Satan disputed over who had rightful possession.

Apparently this was a legal dispute whereby Satan played the traditional role of accuser who was attempting to slander Moses and prove him unworthy of an honorable burial by charging him with murder on the grounds that he had killed the Egyptian in Exodus 2:12.[108]

Judah draws on this interpretive tradition because it was so common during the Second Temple era. Furthermore, as Stern notes, elements of this tradition are found in later Jewish literature as well. *Deuteronomy Rabbah* 11:10 reports a dispute an hour before Moses' death between *Samma'el* – regarded in

---

108. Bauckham, *op. cit.,* 47-48.

Judaism as the angel of death and who is often identified with Satan – and Michael, who on the basis of Daniel 10:13, 21 and 12:1, is regarded as Israel's defender. *Targum Jonathan*, an Aramaic translation and commentary on the prophets, states that Moses' tomb was put under Michael's authority.[109]

As we already noted in the Introduction (see *"Role and Use of Apocryphal Literature"*), although we may not consider such pseudepigraphic sources and traditions authoritative today, at the time the New Testament was being written these various texts and traditions were well-known and considered authoritative by one group or another. We may not know all the reasons why Judah chose to employ these textual interpretations, but they were definitely familiar to his audience, helped support his interpretation of the Tanakh passages, and he believed are clearly applicable to the false teachers he is writing against.

Interpretation/Application (v. 10)

Even though he was one of the archangels, Michael did not dare to bring a charge against the Adversary directly, because he recognized that Satan's role of accuser was given to him by God. Both the Tanakh and the New Testament, along with Jewish tradition, and in line with Job 1-2, do not consider Satan an independent force for evil, but a servant of God with limited authority.[110] Therefore, recognizing that "vengeance is the Lord's (Deut. 32:25; Rom. 12:19), Michael simply says, *"May ADONAI rebuke you,"* echoing God's own words in Zechariah 3:1-2. In contrast, the false teachers whom

---

109. Stern, *op. cit.,* 782.
110. Ibid., 782.

Judah writes against, insult truth, flaunt immorality and mock spiritual authority.

Tanakh Types – Second Set Of Three (v. 11-13)

11 *Woe to them, in that they have walked the road of Cain, they have given themselves over for money to the error of Balaam, they have been destroyed in the rebellion of Korach.*

Judah now applies his second set of three "Tanakh archetypes" (*Cain, Balaam, and Korach)* to these false teachers within his interpretive midrash.

Verses 11-13 amplify Judah's criticism of the false teachers with even greater specificity to their sin, suggesting a group that considered itself more spiritually enlightened and elevated than their fellow believers.[111]

Example Four: Cain

Judah's first example in this second set of fallen Tanakh characters is Cain, originally introduced to us in Genesis 4. Cain was the first of two sons born to Adam and Eve. When Cain and his brother Abel brought offerings before the Lord, Abel's offering was accepted but Cain's was not. This made Cain extremely angry. According to Genesis 4:6-10:

> **6** *ADONAI said to Cain, "Why are you angry? Why so downcast?* **7** *If you are doing what is good, shouldn't you hold your head high? And if you don't do what is good, sin is crouching at the door - it wants you, but you can rule over it."* **8** *Cain had words with Abel his brother; then one time, when they were in the field, Cain turned on Abel his brother and killed him.* **9** *ADONAI said to*

---

111. Kraftchick, *op. cit.,* 45.

*Cain, "Where is Abel your brother?" And he replied, "I don't know; am I my brother's guardian?" **10** He said, "What have you done? The voice of your brother's blood is crying out to me from the ground!*

God warned Cain that his anger would get the best of him if he was not careful to control it. But Cain rebelled against the Lord's warning and eventually killed his brother.

One tradition within post-biblical Judaism depicted Cain's self-love, greed and defiance of God, as the epitome of jealousy, envy and self-indulgence. Although these are generic charges they help make Judah's point.[112]

It is easy to think we are serving God and to assume that we know best when it comes to what God wants from us without having to seek his guidance, instruction, or the council of the community. However, as with Cain, this kind of arrogance is dangerous. In the words of the Torah, *"sin is crouching at the door - it wants you, but you can rule over it."* The choice is ours. We can either continue to rebel against the Lord, or submit to godly council and direction.

Example Five: Balaam

Balaam was a Gentile "seer," or prophet, from *Petor*, a town on the Euphrates River in what is now Syria. According to Numbers 22 he was hired by the Moabite king Balak to curse the people of Israel.

Jewish sages have long debated over who Balaam really was, and whether or not he was a true prophet of God, or simply a sorcerer or magician for hire. Some argue that Balaam was

---

112. Ibid., 46.

a sinister character seeking financial gain (similar to Judah's argument below). Even though God told Balaam not to curse Israel, he still attempted to do so on three separate occasions.

Others, however, argue that Balaam's faith evolved throughout the story – eventually becoming a conduit for blessing Israel. Martin Buber, for instance, took issue with this view. He argued that Balaam was not a true prophet in accordance with the Biblical prophets, and never truly achieved "full prophecy." According to Buber, Balaam was not commissioned by God and therefore did not make decisions on his own. God simply made use of him, despite himself, similar to the way God used Balaam's donkey in Numbers 22.[113]

Judah depicts Balaam as driven by an unquenchable desire for wealth (*"they have given themselves over for money to the error of Balaam ..."*). By doing so, Judah apparently does not primarily rely on the account of Balaam in Numbers 22-24, but on later Jewish exposition of Numbers 31:15-16 which portrays him as a greedy deceptive teacher, whose advice led Israel into immorality:[114]

> **15** *Moshe asked them, "You let the women live?* **16** *Why, these are the ones who - because of Balaam's advice - caused the people of Israel to rebel, breaking faith with ADONAI in the P'or incident, so that the plague broke out among ADONAI's community!*

As a result, Balaam was slain (Numbers 31:8). By connecting Balaam with money, Judah is suggesting that

---

113. Harvey J. Fields, *A Torah Commentary for Our Times: Vol. III* (New York: UAHC Press, 1993), 69.
114. Also see: Josephus, *Antiquities* 1:52-53.

these false teachers whom he is addressing are not motivated by truth, but by money, implying they are insincere and that their teachings should be questioned. They cannot resist the temptation of financial profit.[115]

Many of us can be like Balaam, with moments of stubbornness and resistance to God's will, so caught up in our own plans and desires that we do not even notice God trying to intercept our paths. Balaam heard the Lord's warning and pursued his own choices anyway. When anyone tries to intervene, similar to the way Balaam treated his donkey, we often try to beat them. In the end, through our own stubbornness we are hurting not only ourselves, but those around us.

Balaam's stubbornness and arrogance led to his own spiritual and physical blindness, and eventually to his own downfall. Judah warns that these false teachers face the same defeat, as well as anyone who follows after them.

Example Six: Korach

Judah's final example is that of Korach, who, according to Numbers 16, along with Dothan and Abiram, led 250 people in a rebellion against God's appointed leadership, Moses and Aaron. In the end, they were punished swiftly and terribly—the ground opened up and swallowed them and their households and fire rained down and consumed the 250 others.

Korach was a first cousin of Moses (and also a Levite), and those with him are presented in Numbers 16:3 as having selfish motivations for their rebellion. It seems Korach felt he could do a better job than Moses and Aaron. Therefore, he set out to overthrow them and usurp their authority by assembling

---

115. Kraftchick, *op. cit.,* 46.

a group of people to follow him. Korach, and those with him, rose up and rebelled against Moshe.

Often, like Korach, our envy of others is born out of our own insecurities. Whenever we think we can "do it better," we need to be careful. There are times when it may be true – maybe we can do it better. But the real issue is our motivation. We can definitely be confident in our own abilities, knowing that a mature confidence should never be confused with arrogance.

This is why Judah warns that the fate of these false teachers will be like that of Korach and those with him: *"they have been destroyed in the rebellion of Korach."* It seems these intruders not only taught heresy, but were arrogant, especially toward those in authority. Therefore, Judah's verb choices match the audacity of the original rebellion and underscores that the decree has already been made. Although it may not be as swift as with Korach and his company, it will be just as certain and severe.[116]

Interpretation/Application (v. 12-13)

12 *These men are filthy spots at your festive gatherings meant to foster love; they share your meals without a qualm, while caring only for themselves. They are waterless clouds carried along by the winds; trees without fruit even in autumn, and doubly dead because they have been uprooted;* **13** *savage sea-waves heaving forth their shameful deeds like foam; wandering stars for whom the blackest darkness has been reserved forever.*

According to Kraftchick, in verses 12-13, Judah "uses metaphors drawn from nature to reveal that the speech and

---

116. Ibid., 47.

deeds of the intruders are hollow, mere appearances of truth with no substance." [117] Their conduct will distort the body of believers just as evil warps the natural design of God's creation. Judah uses six graphic metaphors to describe these false teachers:[118]

1) *Filthy spots at your festive gatherings meant to foster love* – the intruders apparently injected their own carousing into holy observances and gatherings, and delighted in their shameless acts.

2) *Shepherds who feed only themselves* – instead of feeding the sheep for whom they are responsible (see Ezek. 34:8-10).

3) *Waterless clouds carried along by the winds* – Like clouds promising much-needed moisture to a parched land, these false-teachers promised soul-satisfying truth, but in reality had nothing of true substance to offer. Also compare with Proverbs 25:14, *"Like clouds and wind that bring no rain is he who boasts of gifts he never gives."*

4) *Trees without fruit even in autumn – doubly dead* – The trees ought to be full with ripe and delicious fruit, instead they are dead and without any life whatsoever.

5) *Savage sea-waves* – as wind-tossed waves often turn up rubbish, so these apostates continually stir up filth (see Is. 57:20).

6) *Wandering stars* – As shooting stars appear in the sky only to fly off into eternal oblivion, so these false teachers are destined for the darkness of eternal hell.

---

117. Ibid., 48.
118. Based on: Burdick and Skilton, *op. cit.,* 1921.

Prophecy Of Enoch (v. 14-16)

14 *Moreover, Enoch, in the seventh generation starting with Adam, also prophesied about these men, saying, "Look! The Lord came with his myriads of holy ones* **15** *to execute judgment against everyone, that is, to convict all the godless for their godless deeds which they have done in such a godless way, and for all the harsh words these godless sinners have spoken against him."* **16** *These people are grumblers and complainers, they follow their evil passions, their mouths speak grandiosities, and they flatter others to gain advantage.*

In the final section of Judah's interpretive midrash he quotes a prophecy found in 1 Enoch 1:9. The prophecy, as quoted here follows a fairly close citation of 1 Enoch 1:9, a passage which survives in both the Greek fragments and Ethiopic version. Later Judaism regarded Enoch as a model of righteousness and as God's friend, and perceived Enoch as a messianic figure.[119]

Judah understands 1 Enoch to be a prophecy about his own time, and specifically about those who are corrupting the believing community. As a result, he changes 1 Enoch's description of God's theophany, his presence seen in a vision, into a prophecy concerning the Messiah's second coming, substituting the noun Κύριος *(kyrios)*, meaning "Lord," instead of 1 Enoch's term "the One" (referring to God). By doing so, Judah is midrashically making use of the ambiguity of the term "Lord" in order to connect Enoch's prophecy with Yeshua.[120]

---

119. Kelly, *op. cit.,* 276.
120. Kraftchick, op. cit., 55.

Verse 14 begins with what seems to be a throw-away reference to Enoch being in the seventh generation from Adam. Although this is already alluded to in Genesis, apparently Judah is referencing an expanded understanding within the Book of Enoch, which he then immediately quotes from. It is possible that Judah mentions Enoch as being in the seventh generation to emphasize a sort of "Enochic lineage" for Yeshua, which was apparently common within early Jewish-believing circles, as explained by Peter J. Tomson:

> "This designation of Enoch [as being 'the seventh from Adam' as stated at Jude 14] can naturally be seen as implied in the story of Genesis (5:1-18); however, the explicit emphasis with which it appears in the apocalypse of Enoch (1 Enoch 93:3, cf. Isa. 60:8) is a different matter ... The Enoch literature contains in any case a tradition of *77 generations* from Adam to the last day.
>
> This counting recurs in a surprising place, namely, in the genealogy of Jesus in Luke (Lk. 3:23-38). If one reckons back via Enoch as the seventh, Abraham as the twenty-first, David as the thirty-fifth, and Joseph, the 'supposed father' of Jesus (v. 23), as the seventy-sixth, one ends up with Jesus being the seventy-seventh from Adam. The Davidic lineage is hereby also confirmed."[121]

This use of numeric genealogical patterns is a common midrashic device. In addition to the Gospel of Luke (as noted above), this type of pattern is also found in the lineage of Yeshua as recorded in Matthew, which also numerically

---

121. Tomson, *op. cit.,* 339.

demonstrates Yeshua's Davidic/Messianic lineage.[122] The point is, as Tomson notes:

> Luke … incorporates traditions, in this case those imprinted by Palestinian-Jewish Enoch motifs. Furthermore, this tradition has the effect of 'grafting' the family tree of Jesus into the line of Enoch, so that he appears as the seventy-seventh generation, during which creation will be renewed. Given that 'Luke' himself wrote approximately two generations later, he must have derived this tradition from 'authoritative' Jewish-Christian circles.[123]

Judah, who is clearly drawing heavily upon apocalyptic and Enochic imagery, apparently believed Yeshua to be the seventieth from Enoch and the seventy-seventh from Adam, thereby affirming his divine status as both Redeemer and Lord. Furthermore, this Enochic reference may have also been another hint to the author's identity as the brother of Yeshua even though he does not explicitly mention it. And if this is truly the case, "It is conceivable that such an Enochic genealogy was cultivated by Jesus' own family members."[124]

In verse 15, the thunderous repetition of the term *"godless,"* used four times in just this one verse, emphasizes Judah's charge against these false teachers, especially leading into the following verse.

In verse 16 he refers directly to their ungodly speech, already referenced in verse 15. Judah's use of "grumblers"

---

122. See specifically Matthew 1:17 and the emphasis on the number 14, representing the Hebrew gamatria of "David," ד (4) ו (6) ד (4) = 14.
123. Tomson, op. cit., 339-340.
124. Ibid., 340.

and "complainers," both of which are only found here in the New Testament, strengthens his critique. After all, the noun "grumblers" is already familiar from the Torah where it is used to describe those Israelites who complained about life in the wilderness after being delivered from Egypt (see, for example, Numbers 14:2, 27, 29, 36).

Apostolic Entreaty (v. 17-19)

17 *But you, dear friends, keep in mind the words spoken in advance by the emissaries of our Lord Yeshua the Messiah.* **18** *They told you, "During the final days there will be scoffers following their own godless passions."* **19** *These are the people who cause divisions. They are controlled by their impulses, because they don't have the Spirit.*

Judah contends that the coming of these godless apostates should not take believers by surprise, for it had been predicted by the Apostles (Acts 20:29; 1 Tim. 4:1; 2 Tim. 3:1-5). His emphasis that *"they told you"* indicates the Apostles' continuous or repeated warning that such godless people would come.[125] He finally concludes that these people are without the Spirit, living and teaching something that is not inspired by the Lord.

Furthermore, the phrase, *"During the final days"* emphasizes the author's apocalyptic worldview,[126] believing he lived in the final days before Messiah's return, something common within the New Testament (Hebrews 1:2, 1 Peter 1:20, Rom. 13:11-12, etc.).

---

125. Burdick and Skilton, *op. cit.,* 1921.
126. Jacobs, *op. cit.,* 462.

Final Encouragement and Appeal (v. 20-23)

20 *But you, dear friends, build yourselves up in your most holy faith, and pray in union with the Ruach HaKodesh.*[127] **21** *Thus keep yourselves in God's love, as you wait for our Lord Yeshua the Messiah to give you the mercy that leads to eternal life.* **22** *Rebuke some who are disputing;* **23** *save others, snatching them out of the fire; and to yet others, show mercy, but with fear, hating even the clothes stained by their vices.*

In contrast to the ungodly false teachers, Judah appeals *"dear friends."* He now focuses his attention on encouraging and engaging his intended audience. He implores them to *"keep yourselves in God's love, as you wait for our Lord Yeshua the Messiah to give you the mercy that leads to eternal life* (v.21).*"*

In verses 22 and 23 Judah pastorally counsels his listeners to bring correction to those who will listen, and thereby save them from the destruction he alluded to above that will come upon the wicked. We are to show mercy toward those who are leading people astray but may be doing so unknowingly or by being deceived themselves. However, we must also demonstrate due diligence and caution. After all, we will know if these people are truly repentant and *"snatched from the fire"* by the spiritual fruit they produce (the kind of holy life they choose to live and in full repentance of their former lifestyle and teachings). Otherwise, spiritual destruction will come to those who knowingly lead others astray.

---

127. Holy Spirit.

Doxology (v. 24-25)

24 *Now, to the one who can keep you from falling and set you without defect and full of joy in the presence of his Sh'khinah*[128] **25** *to God alone, our Deliverer, through Yeshua the Messiah, our Lord - be glory, majesty, power and authority before all time, now and forever. Amen.*

Judah concludes his short letter with a beautiful doxology, which is in effect a liturgical prayer that God will preserve the recipients of the letter from spiritual disaster and false teachings which threaten their final eschatological destinies.[129] However, the closing is without a final message or personal greeting which is customary in New Testament correspondence.

The term δοξολογία *(doxologia)*, from where we get doxology, meaning "glory," is a short hymn of praise often added to the end of certain New Testament books and certain liturgical psalms and hymns. According to many authorities the tradition derives from a similar practice within synagogue liturgy, where versions of the *Kaddish* are used to conclude particular sections of the service. Within Christian liturgical traditions the doxology has largely evolved into meaning only the closing hymn at the end of the service.

Verse 24 begins with a specific reference to God's might, a theme common within Jewish liturgy to this day.[130] N.T. Wright notes that although many translations render the phrase in verse 24 more negatively, *"to keep you from falling;"* the word Judah uses is more positive, *"to keep you un-stumbling."*

---

128. Divine Presence, the manifest glory of God.

129. Bauckham, *op. cit.,* 124.

130. The *Amidah*, one of the central Jewish prayers, opens in a similar way with the second section, *Gevurot*, declaring God's power.

The image is of someone walking along who would have tripped and fallen, but has not done so.[131] The writer is acutely aware of the challenges his readers are exposed to on a daily basis, and therefore, uses this final liturgy to encourage them by emphasizing God alone.

The doxology also reiterates two fundamental themes: the complete integration of belief with actions (a very Jewish/Biblical idea) and the necessity of faithfulness to God's purposes. Furthermore, it emphasizes God's redemptive acts through Yeshua our Messiah. Although the letter seems strong and unyielding, it is based on the reality that God has acted to redeem humanity. Therefore, it is not surprising that those who malign or attempt to hinder that redemption and lead others astray will not receive God's favor. Yet, those who remain faithful will be sustained and rewarded by our God.

---

131. Wright, *op. cit.*, 57.

CONCLUSION

The 25 verses which make up the book of Judah are perhaps the most often neglected within the New Testament. However, there is much more to this little letter than most realize. Although we know that the book became quite popular in the early centuries, we don't know the immediate impact it had on its intended audience. We also do not seem to know how it was perceived by the false teachers Judah was writing against. However, it must have been quite an embarrassment to receive such a public tongue lashing by one of Yeshua's own brothers.

Even for those who organized the canon, Judah's letter was never intended to be insignificant. When especially viewed within its historical Jewish context, it reveals a wealth of knowledge and spiritual truths. As Kraftchick commented, "Jude is not an epistle one reads for comfort or to ponder esoteric questions about theology; it is a letter of challenge. It is a letter of outrage, and we are unaccustomed to this much passion."[132]

Judah warns us to use discernment regarding false-teachers and the abuse of spiritual authority. He also implores

---

132. Ibid., 23.

us to remain faithful in a difficult world. To not give into temptations around us, but to remain focused and true to the "One who keeps us un-stumbling." And for those who are faithful in doing this, eternal rewards await them from our Father in heaven.

Judah's primary concern in the letter, to combat false teaching for the sake and health of the body of Messiah, is finally brought to fruition and appropriately ends with encouragement and acknowledges the eternal greatness of our Lord.

The Epistle of Judah should likewise remind us to live *now* for the return of Messiah. How we live out our faith is far more important than splitting hairs over theology. It is not that doctrine is unimportant for Judah, but that our theologies should shape our interactions with the world, one another, and with God. Every day we should be expecting the return of Messiah … in thought and in deed.

Judah's epistle also teaches us the importance of community. Our lives are intimately linked together with those around us, and false teaching and improper behavior are dangerous because they affect all of us. That is why we must remain focused and committed to one another and producing spiritual fruit.[133]

When this letter was read aloud communally, the hearers would all join together in the concluding *"Amen."*[134] To hear this book read aloud and then responded to so earnestly within the earliest communities of Yeshua-followers must have been quite an experience. Not only is the letter believed to be from

---

133. Galatians 5:22-23.
134. Bauckham, *op. cit.,* 124.

Yeshua's own brother, but it is a scathing condemnation against particular false teachers. May each one of us be careful to heed Judah's warning today and be encouraged to remain faithful despite the pressures and hardships of a difficult world.

APPENDIX:
REFLECTION QUESTIONS

These reflection questions may be used by individuals or in small-group studies to help guide you through the Book of Judah.

1. Who do you think "Judah" is?
   a. After reading the Introduction, do you think the book was actually written by Judah, the brother of Yeshua? Or, do you feel the evidence points toward pseudepigraphic authorship (meaning it was written by an anonymous author and falsely attributed to Judah)?
   b. If the author is really Judah, how and why does it matter? What are the implications if the author is someone else? Does the message or its tone change?

2. Based on the Introduction, to whom do you think Judah was writing? Was it a primarily Gentile audience, a Jewish audience, or a combination of both? Why? What difference might it make, if any?

3. If Judah, the brother of Yeshua, was the actual author, why do you think he chose to write his letter in Greek (if he was a Galilean Jew whose native language was Hebrew/Aramaic)? What are the benefits of writing in Greek?

4. At the time Judah wrote his book, the followers of Yeshua were still predominantly Jewish and they still largely viewed their movement as a sect within Judaism (which they called *"The Way,"* see Acts 22:4, 24:14; cf. 22:20-21). How might this context change the way we should read and study the New Testament? Or should it not? How do you think their worship practices and lifestyles were similar or dissimilar to yours?

5. Why do you think Judah alludes to and quotes from apocryphal sources in his letter?

   a. Do you think by doing so he is claiming any special status for those books?

   b. What do you think is the role of apocryphal sources in general within biblical studies?

   c. Why and how is studying apocryphal literature valuable?

6. Why do you think such notions as fallen angels and battles over Moses' body, for example, became popular in the first century?

7. If the book has historically been largely ignored, why do you think it is still part of our Bibles?

8. Who do you think the false teachers were that Judah was writing about?

   a. Do you think his letter is applicable today?

b. Do we still have false-teachers today? What are the indicators we should look for?

9. How do you think the book of Judah can change your life spiritually?

10. After studying Judah in greater depth, how has your perception of the book changed? Or has it?

GLOSSARY

This glossary contains certain words, phrases and concepts that are regularly used within biblical studies, but which some readers may not be familiar with.

1 Clement – Traditionally attributed to Clement of Rome, it is a letter addressed to the followers of Yeshua in the city of Corinth. The letter dates from the late 1st or early 2nd century, and considered one of the earliest extant Christian documents (along with the Didache) outside of the canonical New Testament.

ADONAI - Literally, "My Lord," a Hebrew word used by Jews to represent the tetragrammaton, the sacred name of God consisting of the four Hebrew letters, *Yud-Hey-Vav-Hey*; but usually as LORD (all capital letters in many Bibles).

Aggadah - From the Aramaic, "to tell," refers to homiletic stories used to make a point, illustrate an idea, or clarify a problem.

Apocrypha – The term comes from the Greek word meaning "hidden" or "secret" and refers to biblical books included in the Septuagint and Vulgate but excluded from Jewish and Protestant canons.

Apocalypse - The term Ἀποκάλυψις *(apocalypsis)* is a Greek word meaning "revelation", an unveiling or unfolding of things previously hidden. As a genre, apocalyptic literature details the authors' visions of the end times as often revealed through a heavenly messenger or Angel.

Apocalyptic – A genre of prophetic writing that developed in post-Exilic Jewish culture, beginning around the third-century BCE. The apocalyptic literature of Judaism and Christianity embraces a considerable period, from the centuries following the Babylonian exile to the close of the Middle Ages.

Barnabas – A non-canonical Greek epistle preserved complete in the 4th century Codex Sinaiticus where it appears at the end of the New Testament.

BCE/CE - The abbreviations BCE and CE, which mean "Before the Common Era" and "Common Era," are commonly used among scholars, and within the Jewish community, instead of the more common BC ("Before Christ") and AD (*"Anno Domini"* which is Latin for "in the year of our Lord").

Canon (Canonical) - From the Greek κανών, meaning "rule" or "measuring stick," and refers to those biblical books that are considered the most authoritative regarding matters of faith, theology and doctrine.

Codex Alexandrinus - A 5th century manuscript of one of the three earliest and most important manuscripts of the Bible in Greek, containing the majority of the Septuagint and the New Testament. Along with the Codex Sinaiticus and the Vaticanus, it is one of the earliest and most complete manuscripts of the Bible.

Codex Sinaiticus – A mid-4ᵗʰ century handwritten copy of the Greek Bible containing the oldest complete copy of the New Testament. Along with the Codex Alexandrinus and the Vaticanus, it is one of the three most important manuscripts of the Bible and considered a celebrated historical treasure.

Codex Vaticanus - One of the oldest extant manuscripts of the Greek Bible (4th century). It is named after its place of conservation in the Vatican Library, where it has been kept since at least the 15th century. Along with the Codex Alexandrinus and the Sinaiticus, it is one of the three most important copies of the Bible.

Dead Sea Scrolls - A collection of manuscripts discovered between 1946 and 1956 at *Khirbet Qumran*. The texts were found inside caves about a mile inland from the northwest shore of the Dead Sea, from which they derive their name. They are considered the most important archaeological find in relation to biblical studies and our understanding of the Second Temple period.

Deuterocanonical – Regarding the books of Scripture contained in the Septuagint but not in the Hebrew and Protestant canons, also known as apocryphal books.

Doxology - The term derives from the Greek word δοξολογία *(doxologia)*, meaning "glory." It refers to a short hymn of praise often added to the end of certain New Testament books and liturgical psalms and hymns. The practice is believed to derive from synagogue liturgy, where versions of the *Kaddish* are used to conclude particular sections of the service. Within Christian liturgical traditions the doxology has largely evolved into meaning only the closing hymn at the end of the service.

Eschatology – Various understandings, discussions or allusions to the End of the Word, the Second Coming, the resurrection of the dead, or the Final Judgment.

Fiscus Iudaicus – A unique Roman tax Jews were forced to pay due to their refusal to participate in the Imperial cult. The Imperial cult identified Roman emperors as divinely sanctioned authorities, and along with its various expected rituals, was inseparable from the worship of Rome's official deities. Jews, and later Christians, found this idea offensive refused to participate in the veneration.

Gamatria - Numerology based on the Hebrew letters. In Hebrew, letters also have a numerical value.

Gnosticism – From the Greek word, *gnôsis*, meaning "knowledge" or "insight." It is the term used for a loosely organized religious and philosophical movement that flourished in the first and second centuries CE. This heresy taught a dualism between a supreme deity and a semi-divine, and lesser-deity, known as the Demiurge, who is associated with the material, physical world. To overcome the material world and rise to the Supreme God, the Gnostic must do so through secret knowledge, which mixed philosophy, metaphysics, curiosity, culture, knowledge, and the secrets of history and the universe.

Hanukkah – Also known as the "Feast of Dedication," celebrates the re-dedication of the Temple in Jerusalem following the victory of the Maccabees over the Syrian-Greek army in the 2nd century BCE. The holiday is also relevant to followers of Yeshua, for according to John 10:22-39, Yeshua also observed Hanukkah.

Jerusalem Council - An early guiding body convened around 50/51 CE made up of the Apostles (Emissaries), Elders, and other prominent figures within the Yeshua-believing community. The purpose of the council, according to Acts 15 and Galatians 2, was to decide whether or not Gentiles must convert to Judaism and, therefore, be obligated to observe all the commandments of the Torah. The final decision, after much debate, was that Gentiles are not required to convert, and therefore, are not obligated to keep most of the commandments. However, they did retain the prohibitions against idolatry, fornication, eating blood, and meat not properly slaughtered (i.e. "strangled," in most English versions) (see Acts 15:10-11 and 19-29).

Kaddish – The Hebrew word *kaddish* (קדיש) is a variation of the root "holy" and refers to a hymn of praise to God found throughout the Jewish prayer service. The central theme of the Kaddish is the magnification and sanctification of God's name. Various versions of the Kaddish are used to conclude particular sections of the service.

Midrash - an interpretive method and a creative body of literature which seeks to "fill-in the gaps" and answer questions within Scripture. It does so through delving into the deeper meaning of words, finding similarities with other biblical passages, and using Hebrew word plays, numerology and parables.

Miryam – The original Hebrew name of Yeshua's mother, Mary.

Nasi - A term regularly used throughout the Hebrew Bible which is often translated as "prince" or "captain." During the Second Temple period (c. 530 BCE – 70 CE) the term was used for the highest ranking member of the Sanhedrin (the great assembly of sages).

Pesher (Pesharim) – A specific type of interpretive (midrashic) literature known from the Dead Sea Scrolls, which is a collection of manuscripts discovered between 1946 and 1956 at *Khirbet Qumran*. The texts were found inside caves about a mile inland from the northwest shore of the Dead Sea, from which they derive their name.

Pseudepigrapha - A genre of non-canonical writings which became especially popular between 200 BCE and 200 CE (and even later). This body of literature claims to have been written by biblical figures and prophets, but was actually written by anonymous authors, and often at a much later time in history than the ascribed figures lived.

Sanhedrin - The council of seventy-one Jewish sages who constituted the Supreme Court and legislative body in Judea during the Roman period.

Semitism – A linguistic term for a characteristic feature of a Semitic language that occurs in another language. This includes the use of certain vocabulary, style and/or syntax influenced by, or borrowed from Hebrew and Aramaic. The most common examples are texts written in Jewish Koine Greek.

Septuagint – Commonly abbreviated as simply LXX, is the earliest Greek translation of the Hebrew Bible (Old Testament) dating to the 3rd and 2nd centuries BCE.

Shepherd of Hermas - A 2nd century work considered canonical scripture by some of the early Church fathers. It had great authority in the 2nd and 3rd centuries.

Shimon - The Hebrew form of the name Simon.

Torah – The word literally means "teaching" or "instruction." It specifically refers to the first five books of the Bible – Genesis, Exodus, Leviticus, Numbers and Deuteronomy. However, it can also be used to refer to Jewish teaching more generally.

Tanakh - Jews refer to our Scriptures as the Tanakh (תנ״ך), which is an acronym for the three primary sections of the Hebrew Bible – the *Torah* (Pentateuch), *Neviim* (Prophets) and *Khetuvim* (Writings). The canon of the Christian Old Testament includes the same books as the Jewish canon, but arranged in a different order.

Ya'akov - The original Hebrew form of the names Jacob and James.

Yehudah – The original Hebrew form of the names Judah, Jude and Judas.

Yosef – The original Hebrew form of the name Joseph.

Yeshua - The earliest followers of Jesus knew him by his original Hebrew name, Yeshua (ישוע), the masculine form of the word for Salvation/Redemption, ישועה).

Zachor – To "remind" or "remember," a central command and concept throughout the Torah. For more on this see the commentary to verses 5-8.

BIBLIOGRAPHY

Barnstone, Willis. *The Restored New Testament.* New York: W.W. Norton & Company, 2009.

Bauckham, Richard J. *Jude, 2 Peter.* World Biblical Commentary 50, Waco: Word Books, 1983.

Boccaccini, Gabriele. "Multiple Judaisms," Bible Review, Vol. XI, Num. I, February 1995, 38-46.

Burdick, Donald W. and John H. Skilton. "Introduction to Jude," *NIV Study Bible.* Grand Rapids: Zondervan, 1985.

Charlesworth, James. Ed. *Jesus' Jewishness.* New York: Crossroad, 1997.

Childs, Brevard S. *Memory and Tradition in Israel.* London: SCM Press, 1962.

Davids, Peter H. "Jude," *Theological Interpretation of the New Testament.* Ed. Kevin J. Vanhoozer. Grand Rapids: Baker Academic, 2005, 229-232.

Enns, Peter. *Inspiration and Incarnation.* Grand Rapids: Baker Academic, 2005.

Fields, Harvey J. *A Torah Commentary for Our Times: Vol. III.* New York: UAHC Press, 1993.

Flusser, David. *The Sage from Galilee.* Grand Rapids: Eerdmans Publishing, 2007.

Isaac, E. "1 (Ethiopic Apocalypse of) Enoch," in *The Old Testament Pseudepigrapha*, Vol. 1. Ed. James H. Charlesworth. Peabody: Hendrickson, 1983, 5-89.

Jacobs, Andrew S. "The Letter of Jude," *The Jewish Annotated New Testament*, Ed. Amy-Jill Levine and Marc Zvi Brettler. New York: Oxford, 2011.

*Jewish Encyclopedia,*1906. "Rome." Accessed April 2, 2014 - http://www.jewishencyclopedia.com/articles/12816-rome#anchor2.

Keener, Craig S. *The IVP Bible Background Commentary: New Testament.* Downers Grove: IVP Academic, 1993.

Kelly, J. N. D. *The Epistles of Peter and of Jude.* Black's New Testament Commentaries, London: Adam & Charles Black, 1969.

Kraftchick, Steven J. *Jude, 2 Peter*. Abingdon New Testament Commentaries, Nashville: Abingdon Press, 2002.

Levine, Amy-Jill. *The Misunderstood Jew.* New York: Harper Collins, 2006.

Merrill, Elmer Truesdell. "The Expulsion of Jews from Rome under Tiberius." *Classical Philology*. Vol. 14, No. 4, (October 1919): 365-372. JSTOR. Accessed April 2, 2014.

Miller, John W. *How the Bible Came to Be.* New York: Paulist Press, 2004.

Priest, J. "Testament of Moses," in *The Old Testament Pseudepigrapha*, Vol.1. Ed. James H. Charlesworth. Peabody: Hendrickson, 1983, 919-934.

Reddish, Mitchell G., Editor. *Apocalyptic Literature: A Reader.* Peabody: Hendrickson, 1990.

Reicke, Bo. *The Epistles of James, Peter and Jude*. The Anchor Bible, New York: Doubleday, 1964.

Stern, David H. *Complete Jewish Bible*. Clarksville: Jewish New Testament Publications, 1998.

_____. *Jewish New Testament Commentary*. Clarksville: Jewish New Testament Publications, 1992.

The Holy Bible: English Standard Version. Wheaton: Crossway, 2002.

Theopedia, "Antinomianism." Accessed March 24, 2014 - http://www.theopedia.com/Antinomianism.

Tomson, Peter J. *'If This Be From Heaven...'* Sheffield: Sheffield Academic Press, 2001.

Vermes, Geza. *Jesus the Jew*. Minneapolis: Fortress Press, 1981.

Whiston, William. *The Works of Josephus: Complete and Unabridged*. Peabody: Hendrickson, 1987.

Wright, N.T. *1 & 2 Peter and Jude*. N.T. Wright for Everyone Bible Study Guides, Downers Grove: Intervarsity Press, 2012.

ABOUT THE AUTHOR

Rabbi Joshua Brumbach is the Senior Rabbi of Ahavat Zion Messianic Synagogue in Beverly Hills, California. He speaks in congregations and conferences around the country and blogs regularly at Yinon Blog *(www.yinonblog.com)*. He has served congregations in Maryland and California and has worked for the Union of Messianic Jewish Congregations (UMJC) and the Messianic Jewish Theological Institute (MJTI).

He is an accredited Jewish educator, has studied in various Jewish institutions including an Orthodox yeshiva in Europe, and is ordained by the UMJC and the Messianic Jewish Rabbinical Council (MJRC). He holds a MJS in Rabbinic Writings from MJTI, a BA in Ancient Near Eastern Civilizations and Biblical Studies from UCLA, and an AA in Anthropology from Mt. Hood Community College.

Additionally, Rabbi Brumbach serves as Vice-President of the Messianic Jewish Rabbinical Council (MJRC), President of the Union of Messianic Believers (UMB), on several committees, including the Theology Committee, of the Union of Messianic Jewish Congregations (UMJC), and on the Administration Committee for the International Messianic Jewish Alliance (IMJA).

He lives in Los Angeles with his wife, Monique, and their toddler son.

OTHER RELATED RESOURCES

Available at Messianic Jewish Resources Int'l. • www.messianicjewish.net
1-800-410-7367
(See website for discounts and specials)

Coming Soon!   ## Complete Jewish Study Bible

-Coming in 2015!
- Introductions and articles by well known Messianic Jewish theologians including Dr. David Friedman, Dr. John Fischer, Dr. Jeffrey Seif, Dr. Dan Juster, Rabbi Russ Resnik, and more.
-Hebrew Idioms found in the New Testament explained by Israeli Messianic Jewish scholar, Dr. David Friedman.

Complete Jewish Bible: *A New English Version*
—Dr. David H. Stern

Presenting the Word of God as a unified Jewish book, the *Complete Jewish Bible* is a new version for Jews and non-Jews alike. It connects Jews with the Jewishness of the Messiah, and non-Jews with their Jewish roots. Names and key terms are returned to their original Hebrew and presented in easy-to-understand transliterations, enabling the reader to say them the way Yeshua (Jesus) did! 1697 pages.

Hardback	978-9653590151	**JB12**	$34.99
Paperback	978-9653590182	**JB13**	$29.99
Leather Cover	978-9653590199	**JB15**	$59.99
Large Print (12 Pt font)	978-1880226483	**JB16**	$49.99

Also available in French and Portuguese.

Jewish New Testament
—Dr. David H. Stern

The New Testament is a Jewish book, written by Jews, initially for Jews. Its central figure was a Jew. His followers were all Jews; yet no other version really communicates its original, essential Jewishness. Uses neutral terms and Hebrew names. Highlights Jewish references and corrects mistranslations. Freshly translated into English from Greek, this is a must read to learn about first-century faith. 436 pages

Hardback	978-9653590069	**JB02**	$19.99
Paperback	978-9653590038	**JB01**	$14.99
Spanish	978-1936716272	**JB17**	$24.99

Also available in French, German, Polish, Portuguese and Russian.

Jewish New Testament Commentary
—Dr. David H. Stern

This companion to the *Jewish New Testament* enhances Bible study. Passages and expressions are explained in their original cultural context. 15 years of research. 960 pages.

Hardback	978-9653590083	**JB06**	$34.99
Paperback	978-9653590113	**JB10**	$29.99

Jewish New Testament on Audio CD or MP3

All the richness of the *Jewish New Testament* beautifully narrated in English by professional narrator/singer, Jonathan Settel. Thrilling to hear, you will enjoy listening to the Hebrew names, expressions and locations as spoken by Messiah.

20 CDs	978-1880226384	**JC01**	$49.99
MP3	978-1880226575	**JC02**	$49.99

Messianic Judaism *A Modern Movement With an Ancient Past*
—David H. Stern

An updated discussion of the history, ideology, theology and program for Messianic Judaism. A challenge to both Jews and non-Jews who honor Yeshua to catch the vision of Messianic Judaism. 312 pages

978-1880226339   **LB62** $17.99

Restoring the Jewishness of the Gospel
A Message for Christians
—David H. Stern

Introduces Christians to the Jewish roots of their faith, challenges some conventional ideas, and raises some neglected questions: How are both the Jews and "the Church" God's people? Is the Law of Moses in force today? Filled with insight! Endorsed by Dr. Darrell L. Bock. 110 pages

English	978-1880226667	**LB70**	$9.99
Spanish	978-9653590175	**JB14**	$9.99

Come and Worship *Ways to Worship from the Hebrew Scriptures*
—Compiled by Barbara D. Malda

We were created to worship. God has graciously given us many ways to express our praise to him. Each way fits a different situation or moment in life, yet all are intended to bring honor and glory to him. When we believe that he is who he says he is [see *His Names are Wonderful!*] and that his Word is true, worship flows naturally from our hearts to his. Softcover, 128 pages.

978-1936716678   LB88 $9.99

His Names Are Wonderful
Getting to Know God Through His Hebrew Names
—Elizabeth L. Vander Meulen and Barbara D. Malda

In Hebrew thought, names did more than identify people; they revealed their nature. God's identity is expressed not in one name, but in many. This book will help readers know God better as they uncover the truths in his Hebrew names. 160 pages.

978-1880226308   **LB58** $9.99

Conveying Our Heritage A Messianic Jewish Guide to Home Practice
—Daniel C. Juster, Th.D. Patricia A. Juster

Throughout history the heritage of faith has been conveyed within the family and the congregation. The first institution in the Bible is the family and only the family can raise children with an adequate appreciation of our faith and heritage. This guide exists to help families learn how to pass on the heritage of spiritual Messianic Jewish life. Softcover, 86 pages

978-1936716739　　LB93　　$8.99

Mutual Blessing *Discovering the Ultimate Destiny of Creation*
—Daniel C. Juster

To truly love as God loves is to see the wonder and richness of the distinct differences in all of creation and his natural order of interdependence. This is the way to mutual blessing and the discovery of the ultimate destiny of creation. Learn how to become enriched and blessed as you enrich and bless others and all that is around you! Softcover, 135 pages.

978-1936716746　　LB94　　$9.99

At the Feet of Rabbi Gamaliel
Rabbinic Influence in Paul's Teachings
—David Friedman, Ph.D.

Paul (Shaul) was on the "fast track" to becoming a sage and Sanhedrin judge, describing himself as passionate for the Torah and the traditions of the fathers, typical for an aspiring Pharisee: "…trained at the feet of Gamaliel in every detail of the Torah of our forefathers. I was a zealot for God, as all of you are today" (Acts 22.3, CJB). Did Shaul's teachings reflect Rabbi Gamaliel's instructions? Did Paul continue to value the Torah and Pharisaic tradition? Did Paul create a 'New' Theology? The results of the research within these pages and its conclusion may surprise you. Softcover, 100 pages.

978-1936716753　　LB95　　$8.99

The Revolt of Rabbi Morris Cohen
Exploring the Passion & Piety of a Modern-day Pharisee
—Anthony Cardinale

A brilliant school psychologist, Rabbi Morris Cohen went on a one-man strike to protest the systematic mislabeling of slow learning pupils as "Learning Disabled" (to extract special education money from the state). His disciplinary hearing, based on the transcript, is a hilarious read! This effusive, garrulous man with an irresistible sense of humor lost his job, but achieved a major historic victory causing the reform of the billion-dollar special education program. Enter into the mind of an eighth-generation Orthodox rabbi to see how he deals spiritually with the loss of everything, even the love of his children. This modern-day Pharisee discovered a trusted friend in the author (a born again believer in Jesus) with whom he could openly struggle over Rabbinic Judaism as well as the concept of Jesus (Yeshua) as Messiah. Softcover, 320 pages.

978-1936716722　　LB92　　$19.99

Debranding God *Revealing His True Essence*
—Eduardo Stein

The process of 'debranding' God is to remove all the labels and fads that prompt us to understand him as a supplier and ourselves as the most demanding of customers. Changing our perception of God also changes our perception of ourselves. In knowing who we are in relationship to God, we discover his, and our, true essence. Softcover, 252 pages.

978-1936716708   LB91 $16.99

Under the Fig Tree *Messianic Thought Through the Hebrew Calendar*
—Patrick Gabriel Lumbroso

Take a daily devotional journey into the Word of God through the Hebrew Calendar and the Biblical Feasts. Learn deeper meaning of the Scriptures through Hebraic thought. Beautifully written and a source for inspiration to draw closer to Adonai every day. Softcover, 407 pages.

978-1936716760   LB96 $25.99

Under the Vine *Messianic Thought Through the Hebrew Calendar*
—Patrick Gabriel Lumbroso

Journey daily through the Hebrew Calendar and Biblical Feasts into the B'rit Hadashah (New Testament) Scriptures as they are put in their rightful context, bringing Judaism alive in it's full beauty. Messianic faith was the motor and what gave substance to Abraham's new beliefs, hope to Job, trust to Isaac, vision to Jacob, resilience to Joseph, courage to David, wisdom to Solomon, knowledge to Daniel, and divine Messianic authority to Yeshua. Softcover, 412 pages.

978-1936716654   LB87 $25.99

The Return of the Kosher Pig *The Divine Messiah in Jewish Thought*
—Rabbi Tzahi Shapira

The subject of Messiah fills many pages of rabbinic writings. Hidden in those pages is a little known concept that the Messiah has the same authority given to God. Based on the Scriptures and traditional rabbinic writings, this book shows the deity of Yeshua from a new perspective. You will see that the rabbis of old expected the Messiah to be divine. Softcover, 352 pages.

978-1936716456   LB81 $ 39.99

Psalms & Proverbs *Tehillim* תְּהִלִּים-*Mishlei* מִשְׁלֵי
—Translated by Dr. David Stern

Contemplate the power in these words anytime, anywhere: Psalms-*Tehillim* offers uplifting words of praise and gratitude, keeping us focused with the right attitude; Proverbs-*Mishlei* gives us the wisdom for daily living, renewing our minds by leading us to examine our actions, to discern good from evil, and to decide freely to do the good. Makes a wonderful and meaningful gift. Softcover, 224 pages.

978-1936716692   LB90 $9.99

Stories of Yeshua
—Jim Reimann, Illustrator Julia Filipone-Erez

Children's Bible Storybook with four stories about Yeshua (Jesus). *Yeshua is Born: The Bethlehem Story* based on Lk 1:26-35 & 2:1-20; *Yeshua and Nicodemus in Jerusalem* based on Jn 3:1-16; *Yeshua Loves the Little Children of the World* based on Matthew 18:1–6 & 19:13–15; *Yeshua is Alive-The Empty Tomb in Jerusalem* based on Matthew 26:17-56, Jn 19:16-20:18, Lk 24:50-53. Ages 3-7, Softcover, 48 pages.

978-1936716685   LB89 $14.99

Matthew Presents Yeshua, King Messiah *A Messianic Commentary*
—Rabbi Barney Kasdan

Few commentators are able to truly present Yeshua in his Jewish context. Most don't understand his background, his family, even his religion, and consequently really don't understand who he truly is. This commentator is well versed with first-century Jewish practices and thought, as well as the historical and cultural setting of the day, and the 'traditions of the Elders' that Yeshua so often spoke about. Get to know Yeshua, the King, through the writing of another rabbi, Barney Kasdan. 448 pages

978-1936716265   **LB76** $29.99

James the Just Presents Application of Torah
A Messianic Commentary
—Dr. David Friedman

James (Jacob) one of the Epistles written to first century Jewish followers of Yeshua. Dr. David Friedman, a former Professor of the Israel Bible Institute has shed new light for Christians from this very important letter.

978-1936716449   LB82 $14.99

To the Ends of the Earth – How the First Jewish Followers of Yeshua Transformed the Ancient World
— Dr. Jeffrey Seif

Everyone knows that the first followers of Yeshua were Jews, and that Christianity was very Jewish for the first 50 to 100 years. It's a known fact that there were many congregations made up mostly of Jews, although the false perception today is, that in the second century they disappeared. Dr. Seif reveals the truth of what happened to them and how these early Messianic Jews influenced and transformed the behavior of the known world at that time.

978-1936716463   LB83 $17.99

Passion for Israel: *A Short History of the Evangelical Church's Support of Israel and the Jewish People*
—Dan Juster

History reveals a special commitment of Christians to the Jews as God's still elect people, but the terrible atrocities committed against the Jews by so-called Christians have overshadowed the many good deeds that have been performed. This important history needs to be told to help heal the wounds and to inspire more Christians to stand together in support of Israel.

978-1936716401   LB78 $9.99

Jewish Roots and Foundations of the Scriptures I
—John Fischer, Th.D, Ph.D.

An outstanding evangelical leader once said: "There is something shallow about a Christianity that has lost its Jewish roots." A beautiful painting is a careful interweaving of a number of elements. Among other things, there are the background, the foreground and the subject. Discovering the roots of your faith is a little like appreciating the various parts of a painting. In the background is the panorama of preparation and pictures found in the Old Testament. In the foreground is the landscape and light of the first century Jewish setting. All of this is intricately connected with and highlights the subject—which becomes the flowering of all these aspects—the coming of God to earth and what that means for us. Discovering and appreciating your roots in this way broadens, deepens and enriches your faith and your understanding of Scripture. This audio is 32 hours of live class instruction - audio is clear and easy to understand.

9781936716623　　**LCD03**　$49.99

The Gospels in their Jewish Context
—John Fischer, Th.D, Ph.D.

An examination of the Jewish background and nature of the Gospels in their contemporary political, cultural and historical settings, emphasizing each gospel's special literary presentation of Yeshua, and highlighting the cultural and religious contexts necessary for understanding each of the gospels. 32 hours of audio/video instruction on MP3-DVD and pdf of syllabus.

978-1936716241　　**LCD01**　$49.99

The Epistles from a Jewish Perspective
—John Fischer, Th.D, Ph.D.

An examination of the relationship of Rabbi Shaul (the Apostle Paul) and the Apostles to their Jewish contemporaries and environment; surveys their Jewish practices, teaching, controversy with the religious leaders, and many critical passages, with emphasis on the Jewish nature, content, and background of these letters. 32 hours of audio/video instruction on MP3-DVD and pdf of syllabus.

978-1936716258　　**LCD02**　$49.99

The Red Heifer *A Jewish Cry for Messiah*
—Anthony Cardinale

Award-winning journalist and playwright Anthony Cardinale has traveled extensively in Israel, and recounts here his interviews with Orthodox rabbis, secular Israelis, and Palestinian Arabs about the current search for a red heifer by Jewish radicals wishing to rebuild the Temple and bring the Messiah. These real-life interviews are interwoven within an engaging and dramatic fictional portrayal of the diverse people of Israel and how they would react should that red heifer be found. Readers will find themselves in the Land, where they can hear learned rabbis and ordinary Israelis talking about the red heifer and dealing with all the related issues and the imminent coming and identity of Messiah.

978-1936716470　　LB79　$19.99

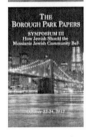

The Borough Park Papers
—Multiple Authors

As you read the New Testament, you "overhear" debates first-century Messianic Jews had about critical issues, e.g. Gentiles being "allowed" into the Messianic kingdom (Acts 15). Similarly, you're now invited to "listen in" as leading twenty-first century Messianic Jewish theologians discuss critical issues facing us today. Some ideas may not fit into your previously held pre-suppositions or pre-conceptions. Indeed, you may find some paradigm shifting in your thinking. We want to share the thoughts of these thinkers with you, our family in the Messiah.

Symposium I:
The Gospel and the Jewish People
248 pages

978-1936716593	LB84	$39.95

Symposium II:
The Deity of Messiah and the Mystery of God
211 pages

978-1936716609	LB85	$39.95

Symposium III:
How Jewish Should the Messianic Community Be?

978-1936716616	LB86	$39.95

On The Way to Emmaus: *Searching the Messianic Prophecies*
—Dr. Jacques Doukhan

An outstanding compilation of the most critical Messianic prophecies by a renowned conservative Christian Scholar, drawing on material from the Bible, Rabbinic sources, Dead Sea Scrolls, and more.

978-1936716432	LB80	$14.99

Yeshua *A Guide to the Real Jesus and the Original Church*
—Dr. Ron Moseley

Opens up the history of the Jewish roots of the Christian faith. Illuminates the Jewish background of Yeshua and the Church and never flinches from showing "Jesus was a Jew, who was born, lived, and died, within first century Judaism." Explains idioms in the New Testament. Endorsed by Dr. Brad Young and Dr. Marvin Wilson. 213 pages.

978-1880226681	**LB29**	$12.99

Gateways to Torah *Joining the Ancient Conversation on the Weekly Portion*
—Rabbi Russell Resnik

From before the days of Messiah until today, Jewish people have read from and discussed a prescribed portion of the Pentateuch each week. Now, a Messianic Jewish Rabbi, Russell Resnik, brings another perspective on the Torah, that of a Messianic Jew. 246 pages.

978-1880226889   **LB42** $15.99

Creation to Completion *A Guide to Life's Journey from the Five Books of Moses*
—Rabbi Russell Resnik

Endorsed by Coach Bill McCartney, Founder of Promise Keepers & Road to Jerusalem: "Paul urged Timothy to study the Scriptures (2 Tim. 3:16), advising him to apply its teachings to all aspects of his life. Since there was no New Testament then, this rabbi/apostle was convinced that his disciple would profit from studying the Torah, the Five Books of Moses, and the Old Testament. Now, Rabbi Resnik has written a warm devotional commentary that will help you understand and apply the Law of Moses to your life in a practical way." 256 pages

978-1880226322   **LB61** $14.99

   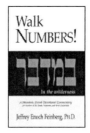 

Walk Genesis!   Walk Exodus!   Walk Leviticus!   Walk Numbers! Walk Deuteronomy!
Messianic Jewish Devotional Commentaries
—Jeffrey Enoch Feinberg, Ph.D.

Using the weekly synagogue readings, Dr. Jeffrey Feinberg has put together some very valuable material in his "Walk" series. Each section includes a short Hebrew lesson (for the non-Hebrew speaker), key concepts, an excellent overview of the portion, and some practical applications. Can be used as a daily devotional as well as a Bible study tool.

Walk Genesis!	238 pages	978-1880226759	**LB34**	$12.99
Walk Exodus!	224 pages	978-1880226872	**LB40**	$12.99
Walk Leviticus!	208 pages	978-1880226926	**LB45**	$12.99
Walk Numbers!	211 pages	978-1880226995	**LB48**	$12.99
Walk Deuteronomy!	231 pages	978-1880226186	**LB51**	$12.99
SPECIAL! Five-book Walk!		5 Book Set **Save $10**	**LK28**	$54.99

Good News According To Matthew
—Dr. Henry Einspruch

English translation with quotations from the Tanakh (Old Testament) capitalized and printed in Hebrew. Helpful notations are included. Lovely black and white illustrations throughout the book. 86 pages.

978-1880226025	**LB03**	$4.99
Also available in Yiddish.	**LB02**	$4.99

They Loved the Torah *What Yeshua's First Followers Really Thought About the Law*
—Dr. David Friedman

Although many Jews believe that Paul taught against the Law, this book disproves that notion. An excellent case for his premise that all the first followers of the Messiah were not only Torah-observant, but also desired to spread their love for God's entire Word to the gentiles to whom they preached. 144 pages. Endorsed by Dr. David Stern, Ariel Berkowitz, Rabbi Dr. Stuart Dauermann & Dr. John Fischer.

978-1880226940 **LB47** $9.99

The Distortion *2000 Years of Misrepresenting the Relationship Between Jesus the Messiah and the Jewish People*
—Dr. John Fischer & Dr. Patrice Fischer

Did the Jews kill Jesus? Did they really reject him? With the rise of global anti–Semitism, it is important to understand what the Gospels teach about the relationship between Jewish people and their Messiah. 2000 years of distortion have made this difficult. Learn how the distortion began and continues to this day and what you can do to change it. 126 pages. Endorsed by Dr. Ruth Fleischer, Rabbi Russell Resnik, Dr. Daniel C. Juster, Dr. Michael Rydelnik.

978-1880226254 **LB54** $11.99

eBooks Now Available!
*All books are available as ebooks
for your favorite reader*

Visit www.messianicjewish.net for direct links to these readers
for each available eBook.

God's Appointed Times *A Practical Guide to Understanding and Celebrating the Biblical Holidays* – **New Edition.**
—Rabbi Barney Kasdan

The Biblical Holy Days teach us about the nature of God and his plan for mankind, and can be a source of God's blessing for all believers–Jews and Gentiles–today. Includes historical background, traditional Jewish observance, New Testament relevance, and prophetic significance, plus music, crafts and holiday recipes. 145 pages.

English	978-1880226353	**LB63**	$12.99
Spanish	978-1880226391	**LB59**	$12.99

God's Appointed Customs *A Messianic Jewish Guide to the Biblical Lifecycle and Lifestyle*
— Rabbi Barney Kasdan

Explains how biblical customs are often the missing key to unlocking the depths of Scripture. Discusses circumcision, the Jewish wedding, and many more customs mentioned in the New Testament. Companion to *God's Appointed Times*. 170 pages.

English	978-1880226636	**LB26**	$12.99
Spanish	978-1880226551	**LB60**	$12.99

Celebrations of the Bible *A Messianic Children's Curriculum*

Did you know that each Old Testament feast or festival finds its fulfillment in the New? They enrich the lives of people who experience and enjoy them. Our popular curriculum for children is in a brand new, user-friendly format. The lay-flat at binding allows you to easily reproduce handouts and worksheets. Celebrations of the Bible has been used by congregations, Sunday schools, ministries, homeschoolers, and individuals to teach children about the biblical festivals. Each of these holidays are presented for Preschool (2-K), Primary (Grades 1-3), Junior (Grades 4-6), and Children's Worship/Special Services. 208 pages.

978-1880226261	**LB55**	$24.99

Passover: *The Key That Unlocks the Book of Revelation*
—Daniel C. Juster, Th.D.

Is there any more enigmatic book of the Bible than Revelation? Controversy concerning its meaning has surrounded it back to the first century. Today, the arguments continue. Yet, Dan Juster has given us the key that unlocks the entire book—the events and circumstances of the Passover/Exodus. By interpreting Revelation through the lens of Exodus, Dan Juster provides a unified overview that helps us read Revelation as it was always meant to be read, as a drama of spiritual conflict, deliverance, and above all, worship. He also shows how this final drama, fulfilled in Messiah, resonates with the Torah and all of God's Word. — Russ Resnik, Executive Director, Union of Messianic Jewish Congregations.

978-1936716210	**LB74**	$10.99

The Messianic Passover Haggadah
Revised and Updated
—Rabbi Barry Rubin and Steffi Rubin.

Guides you through the traditional Passover seder dinner, step-by-step. Not only does this observance remind us of our rescue from Egyptian bondage, but, we remember Messiah's last supper, a Passover seder. The theme of redemption is seen throughout the evening. What's so unique about our Haggadah is the focus on Yeshua (Jesus) the Messiah and his teaching, especially on his last night in the upper room. 36 pages.

English	978-1880226292	**LB57**	$4.99
Spanish	978-1880226599	**LBSP01**	$4.99

The Messianic Passover Seder Preparation Guide
Includes recipes, blessings and songs. 19 pages.

English	978-1880226247	**LB10**	$2.99
Spanish	978-1880226728	**LBSP02**	$2.99

The Sabbath *Entering God's Rest*
—Barry Rubin & Steffi Rubin

Even if you've never celebrated Shabbat before, this book will guide you into the rest God has for all who would enter in—Jews and non-Jews. Contains prayers, music, recipes; in short, everything you need to enjoy the Sabbath, even how to observe havdalah, the closing ceremony of the Sabbath. Also discusses the Saturday or Sunday controversy. 48 pages.

	978-1880226742	**LB32**	$6.99

Havdalah *The Ceremony that Completes the Sabbath*
—Dr. Neal & Jamie Lash

The Sabbath ends with this short, yet equally sweet ceremony called havdalah (separation). This ceremony reminds us to be a light and a sweet fragrance in this world of darkness as we carry the peace, rest, joy and love of the Sabbath into the work week. 28 pages.

	978-1880226605	**LB69**	$4.99

Dedicate and Celebrate!
A Messianic Jewish Guide to Hanukkah
—Barry Rubin & Family

Hanukkah means "dedication" — a theme of significance for Jews and Christians. Discussing its historical background, its modern-day customs, deep meaning for all of God's people, this little book covers all the how-tos! Recipes, music, and prayers for lighting the menorah, all included! 32 pages.

	978-1880226834	**LB36**	$4.99

The Conversation
An Intimate Journal of the Emmaus Encounter
—Judy Salisbury

"Then beginning with Moses and with all the prophets, He explained to them the things concerning Himself in all the Scriptures." Luke 24:27
If you've ever wondered what that conversation must have been like, this captivating book takes you there.

"The Conversation brings to life that famous encounter between the two disciples and our Lord Jesus on the road to Emmaus. While it is based in part on an imaginative reconstruction, it is filled with the throbbing pulse of the excitement of the sensational impact that our Lord's resurrection should have on all of our lives." ~ Dr. Walter Kaiser President Emeritus Gordon-Conwell Theological Seminary. Hardcover 120 pages.

Hardcover	978-1936716173	**LB73**	$14.99
Paperback	978-1936716364	**LB77**	$9.99

Growing to Maturity
A Messianic Jewish Discipleship Guide
—Daniel C. Juster, Th.D.

This discipleship series presents first steps of understanding and spiritual practice, tailored for the Jewish believer. It's purpose is to aid the believer in living according to Yeshua's will as a disciple, one who has learned the example of his teacher. The course is structured according to recent advances in individualized educational instruction. Discipleship is serious business and the material is geared for serious study and reflection. Each chapter is divided into short sections followed by study questions. 256 pages.

978-1936716227	**LB75**	$19.99

Growing to Maturity Primer: *A Messianic Jewish Discipleship Workbook*
—Daniel C. Juster, Th.D.

A basic book of material in question and answer form. Usable by everyone. 60 pages.

978-0961455507	**TB16**	$7.99

Proverbial Wisdom & Common Sense
—Derek Leman

A Messianic Jewish Approach to Today's Issues from the Proverbs Unique in style and scope, this commentary on the book of Proverbs, written in devotional style, is divided into chapters suitable for daily reading. A virtual encyclopedia of practical advice on family, sex, finances, gossip, honesty, love, humility, and discipline. Endorsed by Dr. John Walton, Dr. Jeffrey Feinberg and Rabbi Barney Kasdan. 248 pages.

978-1880226780	**LB35**	$14.99

That They May Be One *A Brief Review of Church Restoration Movements and Their Connection to the Jewish People*
—Daniel Juster, Th.D

Something prophetic and momentous is happening. The Church is finally fully grasping its relationship to Israel and the Jewish people. Author describes the restoration movements in Church history and how they connected to Israel and the Jewish people. Each one contributed in some way—some more, some less—toward the ultimate unity between Jews and Gentiles. Predicted in the Old Testament and fulfilled in the New, Juster believes this plan of God finds its full expression in Messianic Judaism. He may be right. See what you think as you read *That They May Be One*. 100 pages.

978-1880226711	**LB71**	$9.99

The Greatest Commandment
How the Sh'ma Leads to More Love in Your Life
—Irene Lipson

"What is the greatest commandment?" Yeshua was asked. His reply—"Hear, O Israel, the Lord our God, the Lord is one, and you are to love Adonai your God with all your heart, with all your soul, with all your understanding, and all your strength." A superb book explaining each word so the meaning can be fully grasped and lived. Endorsed by Elliot Klayman, Susan Perlman, & Robert Stearns. 175 pages.

978-1880226360	**LB65**	$12.99

Blessing the King of the Universe
Transforming Your Life Through the Practice of Biblical Praise
—Irene Lipson

Insights into the ancient biblical practice of blessing God are offered clearly and practically. With examples from Scripture and Jewish tradition, this book teaches the biblical formula used by men and women of the Bible, including the Messiah; points to new ways and reasons to praise the Lord; and explains more about the Jewish roots of the faith. Endorsed by Rabbi Barney Kasdan, Dr. Mitch Glaser, & Rabbi Dr. Dan Cohn-Sherbok. 144 pages.

978-1880226797	**LB53**	$11.99

You Bring the Bagels, I'll Bring the Gospel
Sharing the Messiah with Your Jewish Neighbor
Revised Edition—Now with Study Questions
—Rabbi Barry Rubin

This "how-to-witness-to-Jewish-people" book is an orderly presentation of everything you need to share the Messiah with a Jewish friend. Includes Messianic prophecies, Jewish objections to believing, sensitivities in your witness, words to avoid. A "must read" for all who care about the Jewish people. Good for individual or group study. Used in Bible schools. Endorsed by Harold A. Sevener, Dr. Walter C. Kaiser, Dr. Erwin J. Kolb and Dr. Arthur F. Glasser. 253 pages.

English	978-1880226650	**LB13**	$12.99
Te Tengo Buenas Noticias	978-0829724103	**OBSP02**	$14.99

Making Eye Contact With God
A Weekly Devotional for Women
—Terri Gillespie

What kind of eyes do you have? Are they downcast and sad? Are they full of God's joy and passion? See yourself through the eyes of God. Using real life anecdotes, combined with scripture, the author reveals God's heart for women everywhere, as she softly speaks of the ways in which women see God. Endorsed by prominent authors: Dr. Angela Hunt, Wanda Dyson and Kathryn Mackel. 247 pages, hardcover.

978-1880226513 **LB68** $19.99

Divine Reversal
The Transforming Ethics of Jesus
—Rabbi Russell Resnik

In the Old Testament, God often reversed the plans of man. Yeshua's ethics continue this theme. Following his path transforms one's life from within, revealing the source of true happiness, forgiveness, reconciliation, fidelity and love. From the introduction, "As a Jewish teacher, Jesus doesn't separate matters of theology from practice. His teaching is consistently practical, ethical, and applicable to real life, even two thousand years after it was originally given." Endorsed by Jonathan Bernis, Dr. Daniel C. Juster, Dr. Jeffrey L. Seif, and Dr Darrell Bock. 206 pages

978-1880226803 **LB72** $12.99

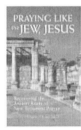

Praying Like the Jew, Jesus
Recovering the Ancient Roots of New Testament Prayer
—Dr. Timothy P. Jones

This eye-opening book reveals the Jewish background of many of Yeshua's prayers. Historical vignettes "transport" you to the times of Yeshua so you can grasp the full meaning of Messiah's prayers. Unique devotional thoughts and meditations, presented in down-to-earth language, provide inspiration for a more meaningful prayer life and help you draw closer to God. Endorsed by Mark Galli, James W. Goll, Rev. Robert Stearns, James F. Strange, and Dr. John Fischer. 144 pages.

978-1880226285 **LB56** $9.99

Growing Your Olive Tree Marriage *A Guide for Couples from Two Traditions*
—David J. Rudolph

One partner is Jewish; the other is Christian. Do they celebrate Hanukkah, Christmas or both? Do they worship in a church or a synagogue? How will the children be raised? This is the first book from a biblical perspective that addresses the concerns of intermarried couples, offering a godly solution. Includes highlights of interviews with intermarried couples. Endorsed by Walter C. Kaiser, Jr., Rabbi Dan Cohn-Sherbok, Jonathan Settel, Dr. Mitchell Glaser & Natalie Sirota. 224 pages.

978-1880226179 **LB50** $12.99

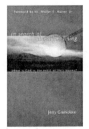

In Search of the Silver Lining *Where is God in the Midst of Life's Storms?*

—Jerry Gramckow

When faced with suffering, what are your choices? Storms have always raged. And people have either perished in their wake or risen above the tempests, shaping history by their responses...new storms are on the horizon. How will we deal with them? How will we shape history or those who follow us? The answer lies in how we view God in the midst of the storms. Endorsed by Joseph C. Aldrich, Ray Beeson, Dr. Daniel Juster. 176 pages.

978-1880226865   LB39 $10.99

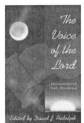

The Voice of the Lord *Messianic Jewish Daily Devotional*

—Edited by David J. Rudolph

Brings insight into the Jewish Scriptures—both Old and New Testaments. Twenty-two prominent Messianic contributors provide practical ways to apply biblical truth. Start your day with this unique resource. Explanatory notes. Perfect companion to the Complete Jewish Bible (see page 2). Endorsed by Edith Schaeffer, Dr. Arthur F. Glaser, Dr. Michael L. Brown, Mitch Glaser and Moishe Rosen. 416 pages.

9781880226704   LB31 $19.99

Kingdom Relationships *God's Laws for the Community of Faith*

—Dr. Ron Moseley

Dr. Ron Moseley's Yeshua: A Guide to the Real Jesus and the Original Church has taught thousands of people about the Jewishness of not only Yeshua, but of the first followers of the Messiah.

In this work, Moseley focuses on the teaching of Torah -- the Five Books of Moses -- tapping into truths that greatly help modern-day members of the community of faith.

The first section explains the relationship of both the Jewish people and Christians to the Kingdom of God. The second section lists the laws that are applicable to a non-Jew living in the twenty-first century and outside of the land of Israel.

This book is needed because these little known laws of God's Kingdom were, according to Yeshua, the most salient features of the first-century community of believers. Yeshua even warned that anyone breaking these laws would be least in the Kingdom (Matt. 5:19). Additionally, these laws will be the basis for judgment at the end of every believer's life. 64 pages.

978-1880226841   LB37 $8.99

Train Up A Child *Successful Parenting For The Next Generation*

—Dr. Daniel L. Switzer

The author, former principal of Ets Chaiyim Messianic Jewish Day School, and father of four, combines solid biblical teaching with Jewish sources on child raising, focusing on the biblical holy days, giving fresh insight into fulfilling the role of parent. 188 pages. Endorsed by Dr. David J. Rudolph, Paul Lieberman, and Dr. David H. Stern.

978-1880226377   LB64 $12.99

Fire on the Mountain - *Past Renewals, Present Revivals and the Coming Return of Israel*

—Dr. Louis Goldberg

The term "revival" is often used to describe a person or congregation turning to God. Is this something that "just happens," or can it be brought about? Dr. Louis Goldberg, author and former professor of Hebrew and Jewish Studies at Moody Bible Institute, examines real revivals that took place in Bible times and applies them to today. 268 pages.

978-1880226858   LB38 $15.99

Voices of Messianic Judaism *Confronting Critical Issues Facing a Maturing Movement*

—General Editor Rabbi Dan Cohn-Sherbok

Many of the best minds of the Messianic Jewish movement contributed their thoughts to this collection of 29 substantive articles. Challenging questions are debated: The involvement of Gentiles in Messianic Judaism? How should outreach be accomplished? Liturgy or not? Intermarriage? 256 pages.

978-1880226933   LB46 $15.99

The Enduring Paradox *Exploratory Essays in Messianic Judaism*

—General Editor Dr. John Fischer

Yeshua and his Jewish followers began a new movement—Messianic Judaism—2,000 years ago. In the 20th century, it was reborn. Now, at the beginning of the 21st century, it is maturing. Twelve essays from top contributors to the theology of this vital movement of God, including: Dr. Walter C. Kaiser, Dr. David H. Stern, and Dr. John Fischer. 196 pages.

978-1880226902   LB43 $13.99

The World To Come *A Portal to Heaven on Earth*

—Derek Leman

An insightful book, exposing fallacies and false teachings surrounding this extremely important subject... paints a hopeful picture of the future and dispels many non-biblical notions. Intriguing chapters: Magic and Desire, The Vision of the Prophets, Hints of Heaven, Horrors of Hell, The Drama of the Coming Ages. Offers a fresh, but old, perspective on the world to come, as it interacts with the prophets of Israel and the Bible. 110 pages.

978-1880226049   LB67   .$9.99

Hebrews Through a Hebrew's Eyes

—Dr. Stuart Sacks

Written to first-century Messianic Jews, this epistle, understood through Jewish eyes, edifies and encourages all. 119 pages. Endorsed by Dr. R.C. Sproul and James M. Boice.

978-1880226612   LB23 $10.99

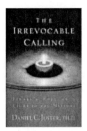

The Irrevocable Calling *Israel's Role As A Light To The Nations*
—Daniel C. Juster, Th.D.

Referring to the chosen-ness of the Jewish people, Paul, the Apostle, wrote "For God's free gifts and his calling are irrevocable" (Rom. 11:29). This messenger to the Gentiles understood the unique calling of his people, Israel. So does Dr. Daniel Juster, President of Tikkun Ministries Int'l. In *The Irrevocable Calling*, he expands Paul's words, showing how Israel was uniquely chosen to bless the world and how these blessings can be enjoyed today. Endorsed by Dr. Jack Hayford, Mike Bickle and Don Finto. 64 pages.

978-1880226346 **LB66** $8.99

Are There Two Ways of Atonement?
—Dr. Louis Goldberg

Here Dr. Louis Goldberg, long-time professor of Jewish Studies at Moody Bible Institute, exposes the dangerous doctrine of Two-Covenant Theology. 32 pages.

978-1880226056 **LB12** $ 4.99

Awakening *Articles and Stories About Jews and Yeshua*
—Arranged by Anna Portnov

Articles, testimonies, and stories about Jewish people and their relationship with God, Israel, and the Messiah. Includes the effective tract, "The Most Famous Jew of All." One of our best anthologies for witnessing to Jewish people. Let this book witness for you! Russian version also available. 110 pages.

English	978-1880226094	**LB15**	$ 6.99
Russian	978-1880226018	**LB14**	$ 6.99

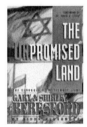

The Unpromised Land *The Struggle of Messianic Jews Gary and Shirley Beresford*
—Linda Alexander

They felt God calling them to live in Israel, the Promised Land. Wanting nothing more than to live quietly and grow old together in the country of refuge for all Jewish people, little did they suspect what events would follow to try their faith. The fight to make *aliyah*, to claim their rightful inheritance in the Promised Land, became a battle waged not only for themselves, but also for Messianic Jews all over the world that wish to return to the Jewish homeland. Here is the true saga of the Beresford's journey to the land of their forefathers. 216 pages.

978-1880226568 **LB19** $ 9.99

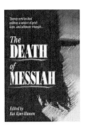

Death of Messiah *Twenty fascinating articles that address a subject of grief, hope, and ultimate triumph.*
—Edited by Kai Kjaer-Hansen

This compilation, written by well-known Jewish believers, addresses the issue of Messiah and offers proof that Yeshua—the true Messiah—not only died, but also was resurrected! 160 pages.

978-1880226582   **LB20** $ 8.99

Beloved Dissident *(A Novel)*
—Laurel West

A gripping story of human relationships, passionate love, faith, and spiritual testing. Set in the world of high finance, intrigue, and international terrorism, the lives of David, Jonathan, and Leah intermingle on many levels--especially their relationships with one another and with God. As the two men tangle with each other in a rising whirlwind of excitement and danger, each hopes to win the fight for Leah's love. One of these rivals will move Leah to a level of commitment and love she has never imagined--or dared to dream. Whom will she choose? 256 pages.

978-1880226766   **LB33** $ 9.99

Sudden Terror
—Dr. David Friedman

Exposes the hidden agenda of militant Islam. The author, a former member of the Israel Defense Forces, provides eye-opening information needed in today's dangerous world.

Dr. David Friedman recounts his experiences confronting terrorism; analyzes the biblical roots of the conflict between Israel and Islam; provides an overview of early Islam; demonstrates how the United States and Israel are bound together by a common enemy; and shows how to cope with terrorism and conquer fear. The culmination of many years of research and personal experiences. This expose will prepare you for what's to come! 160 pages.

978-1880226155   **LB49** $ 9.99

It is Good! *Growing Up in a Messianic Family*
—Steffi Rubin

Growing up in a Messianic Jewish family. Meet Tovah! Tovah (Hebrew for "Good") is growing up in a Messianic Jewish home, learning the meaning of God`s special days. Ideal for young children, it teaches the biblical holidays and celebrates faith in Yeshua. 32 pages to read & color.

978-1880226063   **LB11** $ 4.99